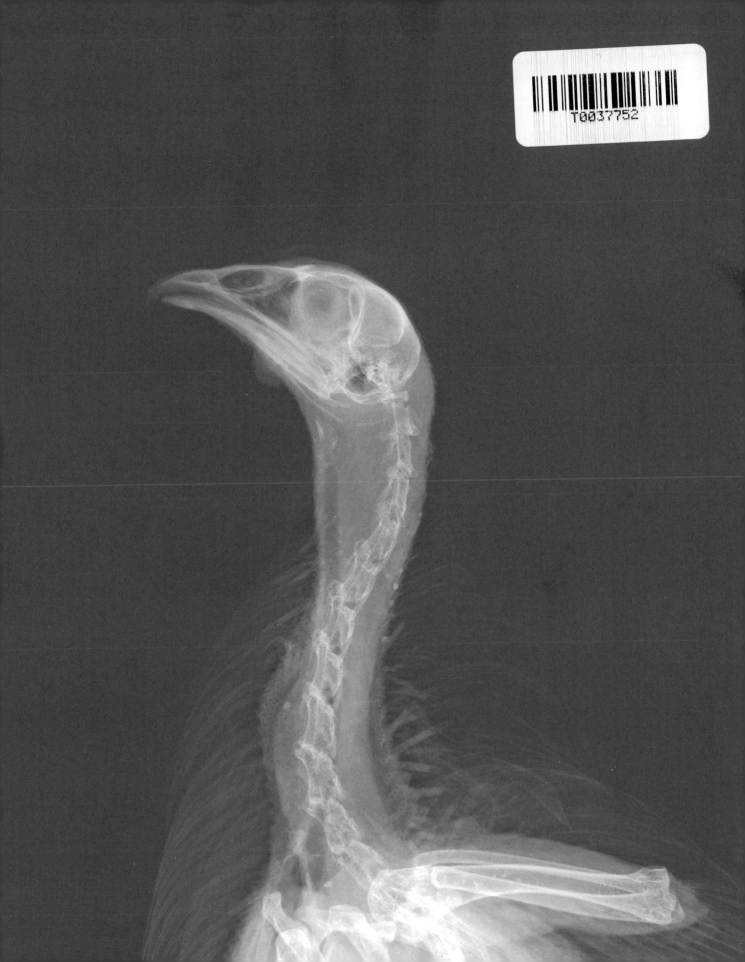

T0037752

INSIDE IN

X-Rays of Nature's Hidden World

Jan Paul Schutten

PHOTOGRAPHY BY **Arie van 't Riet**

TRANSLATION BY **Laura Watkinson**

GREYSTONE KIDS

GREYSTONE BOOKS • VANCOUVER/BERKELEY

Contents

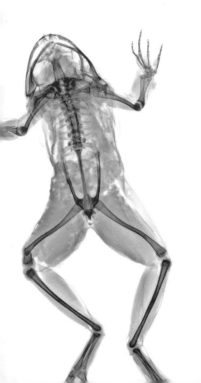

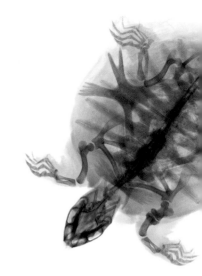

Birds

Mammals

First, a few words ...

This book is more special than you might think.

Take a look in a bookstore or a library: you won't find many books of X-ray photographs. After all, it's not easy for just anyone to get access to an X-ray machine, and then there are strict safety guidelines that have to be followed. Even so, Arie van 't Riet has managed to create a huge number of these amazing, beautiful X-ray pictures.

It all started because Arie worked in a hospital for years, where he helped to take lots and lots of X-ray photographs. But the pictures for this book were not taken in a hospital. They were made in his own workshop. That's pretty unusual, because taking X-ray photos can be risky. If you take a picture of teeth or a broken bone once or twice, not much can go wrong. But if you do it over and over again, the level of radiation that you are exposed to can become dangerous. So the room where you take the photos has to be completely safe. For that reason, there are different government regulations, depending on where you live, about who can and can't use the X-ray machinery. You also need to have a good reason: you probably won't be allowed to take X-ray pictures just for fun.

Years ago, when the people at Arie's hospital had an X-ray machine they didn't need anymore, Arie asked if he could have it. That way, he could practice in his workshop and learn to take even better pictures. Arie made sure that his workshop met all the safety requirements.

Now, with his own X-ray machine, Arie could look at all kinds of things that wouldn't normally be examined in a hospital. For example, art collectors consulted him to see if their paintings were genuine. An X-ray machine allows you to peek under the bottom layer of paint, so you can find out if the painting was actually made in the way painters used to work in the past. Other people took their broken headphones to Arie, and he used his X-ray photos to pinpoint exactly where the break in the cable was. However, what Arie really wanted to do was take pictures of animals and flowers.

Arie was interested in the difference between hard and soft objects when exposed to X-rays, so he improved his technique by photographing subjects such as an animal with thick fur next to a delicate little flower. Not only did this teach him to take better photographs, but he also discovered what a special combination that could be. That inspired him to create X-ray photographs that were as beautiful as he could make them.

Arie obviously wanted to practice with as many different kinds of animals as he could, but getting hold of subjects was tricky. Finding insects wasn't a problem, and he could easily buy fish. But what about the rest? He couldn't work with live animals—it would be wrong to expose them to harmful X-rays, and anyway, how would he keep them still long enough to take the photograph? And he certainly didn't want to kill any animals to make this book.

You might imagine it would be simple to go out to the countryside and find animals there, but wild animals are often protected by law, even if they're dead. Arie had to report every creature he found before he was allowed to take it home, even the little ones. He found a lot of the animals dead at the side of the road, and sometimes he bought them from taxidermists, who stuff animals for display. Most of the reptiles came from owners who gave their dead pets to Arie. He's one of the very few people who are delighted to receive a dead animal as a gift.

All the photographs in this book are real. Arie obviously designed special layouts to make them more interesting, and he added a bit of color to the black-and-white pictures. Otherwise, though, everything you see is exactly as it looked in real life. You can see every tooth, every bone, every skull just as it was, without any computer editing. So sometimes you'll notice that an insect wing is no longer completely perfect, or a prawn's leg is a bit broken, or a flower is missing a petal or two. But that's all part of nature, and it makes the photographs even more beautiful.

When Arie sent me his photographs, I knew they would make a very special book, so I was happy to write the words to go with them. These descriptions will give you some extra information about the animals, so that you know what you're looking at. But they're really meant to make you look more closely at the photographs, because now you have the chance to see what is normally hidden. And you need to seize that chance—with both eyes!

—Jan Paul Schutten, Amsterdam

Hey, wait a minute.
What exactly are X-ray photographs?

X-ray radiation is electromagnetic radiation. That might sound complicated, but the light you see around you is also electromagnetic radiation. Light doesn't go straight through you though—but X-rays do. That's because X-rays have a higher energy. You can compare it to jumping into water. If you jump into the swimming pool from the side, then you don't go too deep into the water. But if you jump from the high diving board, you have more energy when you reach the water, so you go way deeper. You can picture the effect of X-rays in the same way.

X-rays don't have so much energy that they can go all the way through everything though. The radiation from an X-ray machine is blocked by tough materials, such as bones and teeth. That's why you can look at an X-ray picture to see if you've broken a bone.

Taking X-ray photographs works differently from ordinary photos. To create an image, the radiation actually has to pass through your body. You need an X-ray machine that emits the radiation, then the person or object you're photographing, and behind that X-ray film to receive the radiation and turn it into an X-ray photograph. The areas that block the radiation show up as light, and the rest is dark. Then, if you want, you can use a computer to reverse the black and white, so the bones show up as dark and the soft parts are light.

When you make X-ray photos, you can play around with the amount of energy that you give to the radiation. The higher the energy, the more easily the radiation passes through something. So if you want to take an X-ray picture of a hard material, you use X-ray radiation with high energy. For soft or thin materials, on the other hand, you need X-ray radiation with low energy. What makes Arie so smart is that he knows how to use exactly the right combination of high and low energies to capture both thin flower petals and hard bones and teeth in the same shot.

Good. Now we can finally get started on the photographs!

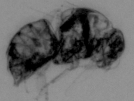

ARTHROPODS
AND MOLLUSKS

THE SCORPION
What a cutie!

The world isn't fair. All a bear cub has to do is be born and everyone says, "Ohhhh! Woooow! It's such a cutie!" But no one is ever going to think this scorpion is cute, because it looks pretty scary.

It isn't really that scary though. Its distant ancestors—yes, *they* were scary. Around 430 million years ago, there were scorpions roaming the Earth that were over 3 feet (1 meter) long. But this little critter? Aww, come on. It's cute! Right? No? Well, maybe you'll think it's a bit nicer when you know more about it. For example, which group of animals do you think the scorpion is most closely related to? Arachnids, like the tarantula? Insects, like flies and wasps? Or crustaceans, like lobsters and crabs? Don't answer right away. Take a good look first.

Cover the long tail with your fingers. And cover those huge front legs with your other hand. What kind of animal do you see now? That's right! Scorpions are more closely related to spiders than to lobsters. Huh? But spiders don't have ten legs—they have eight, don't they? Yup. And so does this scorpion. The "front legs" with those scary pincers aren't actually legs at all—they're feelers. Technically, they're called pedipalps. They begin at the side of the creature's mouth, not alongside the body like real legs. The tarantula, the scorpion's distant relative, also has two similar bits sticking out from its head. Those are pedipalps too.

Are scorpions dangerous? Yes! Well, if you're a grasshopper or a cockroach, they are. The scorpion uses venom from the stinger at the end of its tail to eliminate its prey at lightning speed. But if you're a human, they won't do you much harm. They'll never just sting you for no reason. They only sting when they feel cornered. And there are hundreds of species of scorpions, but only a handful are fatal to humans. In most cases, a sting from a scorpion is no worse than a sting from a bee or a wasp.

So do you like scorpions a bit more now? No? Well, what if I told you the scorpion mom takes great care of all her many, many little ones and carries them around on her back until they're big enough to look after themselves? You still don't like them? Really? Hmm, you know, maybe you have a point.

THE GIANT PRAWN
Underwater knights

Giant prawns are swimming knights, well protected inside their sturdy stainless-steel armor and equipped with long, deadly whips. Actually, those are completely harmless feelers, but that's beside the point. What matters is that, unlike humans, prawns have their skeletons on the outside while with us it's on the inside. As you can see, there's not one single bit of bone or protection inside their bodies. Weird? Nope. The vast majority of animals on our planet have outer armor instead of an inside skeleton— prawns and scorpions, but also spiders, wasps, flies, and all the other insects. And how about slugs and snails?

You might be wondering now why we carry our protection on the inside. Imagine if your skull were on the outside, like a helmet. Then a bang on the head would be a lot less painful, wouldn't it? Or what if, instead of ribs, we had a bulletproof vest that protected our heart and lungs? Handy, huh? But . . . how many times have you ever needed a bulletproof vest? Hopefully never. And when you remember that those things can easily weigh 5 or 6 pounds (2 or 3 kilograms), it could be more of a hindrance than a help. Bear in mind that a real knight's armor is incredibly heavy. Also, when you grow, your armor would have to grow along with you. So all those armored animals have to shed their old layer while they grow a new, bigger, heavier one. What a bother. So, when you think about it, we're actually put together pretty well, and we don't have much to complain about. And the prawns are happy too, because they need protection way more than they need bones.

This does make the prawn less suitable for X-rays, unfortunately, as an external skeleton means there's not much to be seen on the inside. X-rays pass straight through the soft parts and are blocked by the tough body parts, such as bones. So we can't see too much new here—apart from the dark line running along the body all the way to the tail. That's the prawn's gut. The gut is soft too, but the poop inside it is full of little solid bits of food, and they stop the X-rays so the gut stands out clearly. A prawn's gut might look very long, but so is ours. In humans, though, it's all coiled up inside our abdomen.

There's not much else to see inside. So maybe we should take a closer look at the legs. Prawns are a member of the order Decapoda, creatures with ten feet. Go ahead and count them. Tricky, huh? Ten? Nope! Prawns actually have twenty legs! There are five pairs of long ones at the front and five pairs of smaller ones at the back. But what good are legs in the water? You don't need to walk in the water, and aren't fins more useful for swimming?

Well, guess what! They're not all legs for walking. The prawn's back legs are a special kind of "swimming legs," more like fins. And if you subtract those ten fins from the twenty legs, then you're back to ten. But then what do they use their *real* legs for? Yes, they're for walking. Prawns do that when they're exploring the bottom, and they also use them for grabbing and for digging. When they're taking a little break, they like to sit under the sand, where they're invisible. Because their armor protects the prawns from lots of predators, but not from all of them. There are still plenty of creatures that can swallow a prawn whole, complete with its shell.

It might be fun to have all those legs, but if none of them are strong enough to hold a sword or shield, you'd be a pretty useless knight.

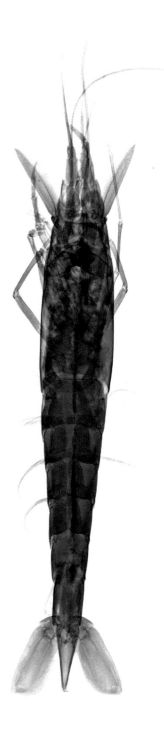

THE BUMBLEBEE
Buzzing hourglasses

Fashions come and go, and at one time it was considered stylish for women to have a tiny waist. To get that look, they would lace themselves into tight corsets to make their waists as small as possible (even if they couldn't breathe!). This look was described as a "wasp waist." That's because the wasp is famous in the insect world for its very narrow waist. Compare the creature in this photo to a big fat bumblebee. There's quite a difference, huh?

Well, actually, no. That's why it's great that we have X-ray photos. Because what you're looking at in this photo is not a wasp. It's a bumblebee! Bumblebees have just as much of a "wasp waist" as wasps do. Their woolly fur just makes them look quite a bit chunkier than they really are.

It's impossible for a person to have a disappearing waist like these insects, and that's a good thing, because this feature makes them very vulnerable. Their lower bodies and their chest sections are joined together by just a few tiny muscles and a very small piece of external skeleton. It's the same story with their heads and their bodies. In fact, they're basically three loosely dangling body parts.

So it's not that great to be a bumblebee. Although they do have one thing we should envy: the antennae on their heads. They're thousands of times smaller than a smartphone, and yet bees can use them to feel, taste, hear, and smell. What did you say? No, they can't use them to connect to Wi-Fi. That's not a problem for bumblebees though, because they're more interested in nectar than in Netflix.

THE DRAGONFLY
Born stunt pilots

Aircraft builders have constructed jets that can reach speeds of 4,400 miles per hour (7,000 kilometers per hour). They have made planes that can fly around the world without refueling, and planes that are invisible to radar, and planes that can transport 500 passengers. But no one has ever designed a plane that can do what a dragonfly can. All those engineers must be green with envy. Because, as quick as lightning, dragonflies can dart forward, backward, up, down, left, right—within just a second, they can change direction several times. Try doing that with a jet fighter. They are also among the fastest insects in the skies—and some of the keenest globe-trotters: there's one kind of dragonfly that can travel a distance of thousands of miles in a single migration.

Dragonflies are miracles of technology. You can already see some of that in the photo. The secret is in their four wings. You see those two thick black lines in the dragonfly's upper body? Those are super-strong flying muscles. They use them to control their wings independently of each other, so that they can get up to all kinds of flying antics in the air. The long tail is there to help them keep their balance during all those flying maneuvers. Otherwise their bodies would go shooting off in all directions when they were performing their stunts.

You might think the dragonfly would need a big brain to control such complicated flying movements, but that's not the case. Just take a look at that head—their cockpit is made up mainly of eyes. So they can see fantastically well. Their prey doesn't stand a chance against all that sight and flight power. Young dragonflies don't even take flying lessons before they start performing aerial acrobatics. First, as larvae, with a short, wingless body and smaller eyes, they putter around in the water for months. Then one day they unwrap themselves, like a gift to the world. The head breaks through the larva shell, and then the wings, and the tail parts slide out like a telescope—they're ready to explore the sky!

And now for the good news: these stunt pilots are on our side. They fight with us against our greatest enemy on Earth. No, not tigers or crocodiles. Mosquitoes! Mosquitoes carry diseases like malaria, which kill more people than all the great predators combined. And a big dragonfly can eat hundreds of these disease-carriers in a day. Long live the dragonfly! But don't they sting people too? No, that's a stubborn myth. They're not even capable of hurting us, because they don't have a stinger, and their mouths are barely strong enough to bite through our skin. They're much more interested in their prey, which they nimbly grab from the air with their legs. Because as well as four wings, they have six legs—those are the straw-like things you can see on their upper body.

It's not surprising that dragonflies are so very cleverly put together. Time was on their side. They have already had around 300 million years to develop and improve their design. Aircraft builders, in comparison, are still at the drawing-board stage. Who know what *they'll* have come up with in another 300 million years?

THE BUTTERFLY
Bodybuilding caterpillars

If you see a butterfly in the wild, the glamour of its striking wings instantly captures all of your attention. With those bright colors, they're like flying billboards. However, in an X-ray photograph you don't see the colors. So this photo is a perfect opportunity to focus on other things for once. For example, do you see how big those wings are compared to the body? After starting life as a caterpillar, butterflies have to develop a lot of muscles to get those wings moving. That's why a butterfly's body looks completely different from a caterpillar's. It's as if the butterfly spent time working out while it was still inside its cocoon, pumping iron to get a bodybuilder's physique. Of course, it helps that its wings are so light. Otherwise it could work out for a thousand hours and still not be able to move them.

A butterfly's wings might be light, but they're still pretty strong. That's because they have a very clever design. See those lines all over the wings? Those are the butterfly's wing veins. When the butterfly emerges from its cocoon, those veins are pumped full of blood, which keeps the wings taut. If you think about it, it's like an inflatable boat that stays firm when you pump air into it. And if a small piece of wing tears, those strong veins will prevent the wing from becoming even more damaged. It works a bit like a stained-glass window. If you throw a stone through an ordinary window, the whole pane of glass breaks. A stained-glass window, however, remains intact, except for that one broken section. That's how it works with butterflies too, and that's important, because a broken bit of butterfly wing never becomes whole again.

The butterfly's wings are not just there for flying with, by the way. They also act as solar panels. Butterflies don't like cold weather. If their body temperature drops below 82 degrees Fahrenheit (28 degrees Celsius), they can't fly anymore. As soon as the sun shines on their wings though, the warm blood from the wing veins flows to the muscles to get them moving again. Useful, huh?

You see, that's the sort of fact you miss out on when you only pay attention to the pretty patterns on their wings.

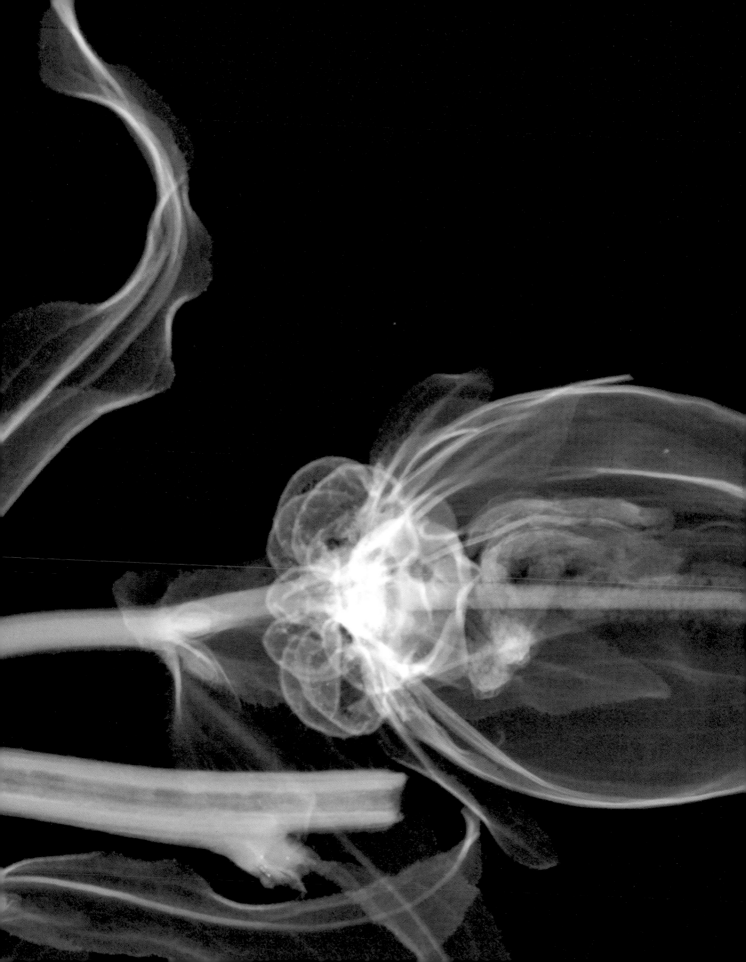

THE CENTIPEDE
A head with legs

Whoever came up with the name "centipede" was either very good at exaggerating or very bad at counting. Because the name means that this insect has 100 feet, but you can count the legs in the photo on the right as many times as you like, and you won't find more than 32. Some species, such as the one in the photo on the left, have quite a lot of extra legs, but they still don't make it to anything like 100 either.

The front pair of legs, close to the head, can barely be seen. Those are the legs you need to look out for though, because they're venomous, and centipedes can bite with them, which can be pretty painful. But hang on a minute . . . if their legs start near the head, then where is their upper body? Nowhere! A centipede is just a head with legs. But it's a dangerous head with legs.

What lions and tigers are to humans, centipedes are to the insect world: predators that are both fast and deadly. They don't just pick on insects either—they also go after snails, worms, and each other. There are even centipedes living in the desert that eat small rodents. Of course, there are also animals that have centipedes on their menu, such as birds. But centipedes are not very easy to catch. You can see, for example, that their back legs are pretty long. They look almost like the antennae on their heads. With some kinds of centipedes, you can hardly tell one end from the other, so attackers can easily make a mistake. And if they go for the wrong end, they can get bitten by the venomous legs at the head end.

Centipedes have another trick too: if a bird grabs them by their legs, they can quickly detach them from their bodies and run away. So the bird is left with just a beakful of legs. Not only do the centipedes still have enough legs to walk with, but the limbs they lost grow back again. Hmm . . . and if that happens over and over and over again, then maybe they *can* end up with 100 legs after all.

THE SNAIL
The mushiest mollusk

"Sit still, Tarzan!" "Stay, Toffie!" "Stop scratching, Bear!" If you've ever tried to take a photo of your dog or cat, you'll know how difficult it is. They never sit still, and right at the moment you want to take the picture, they run away. It's even harder if you're trying to take an X-ray photo, because then the animal is not allowed to move at all for a really long time. None of these photos are of living animals, but if you wanted to try taking X-ray photos of one, at least with a slow-moving snail you might have a fighting chance!

What exactly can you see in this photograph? This is another example of an animal with a tough exterior and a soft interior. It doesn't get much mushier than this mollusk. Snails have a heart, but you can't see that. They have a kidney, but you can't see that. They have a stomach, but you can't see that either. In fact, you can't see one single organ, except for their eyes, sitting on their tentacles, and the foot, the organ they use to move along. Yes, it's a nice photo, but otherwise completely pointless, right?

Look again, though. If you know where the organs are, then you might notice something. Those organs are precisely in the part of their body that's protected by the shell. So the most important parts have the best protection. The same is true for humans: our hearts are behind tough ribs, and our brains are completely covered by a thick skull. Brains are less important for snails than they are for us, so their brains are unprotected inside their heads. And their lack of speed means they don't need to wear a helmet anyway.

Otherwise, humans and snails are pretty different. For example, snails have a separate organ that their protection grows out of: it's called the mantle. Slugs grow just a thin shield, while snails make a complete house. We have no mantle, and that's just as well. How would you like to find a kitchen suddenly growing on your thigh? Or a bedroom on your back? Yeah, I thought not!

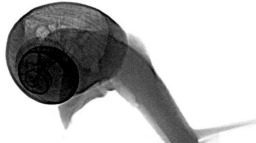

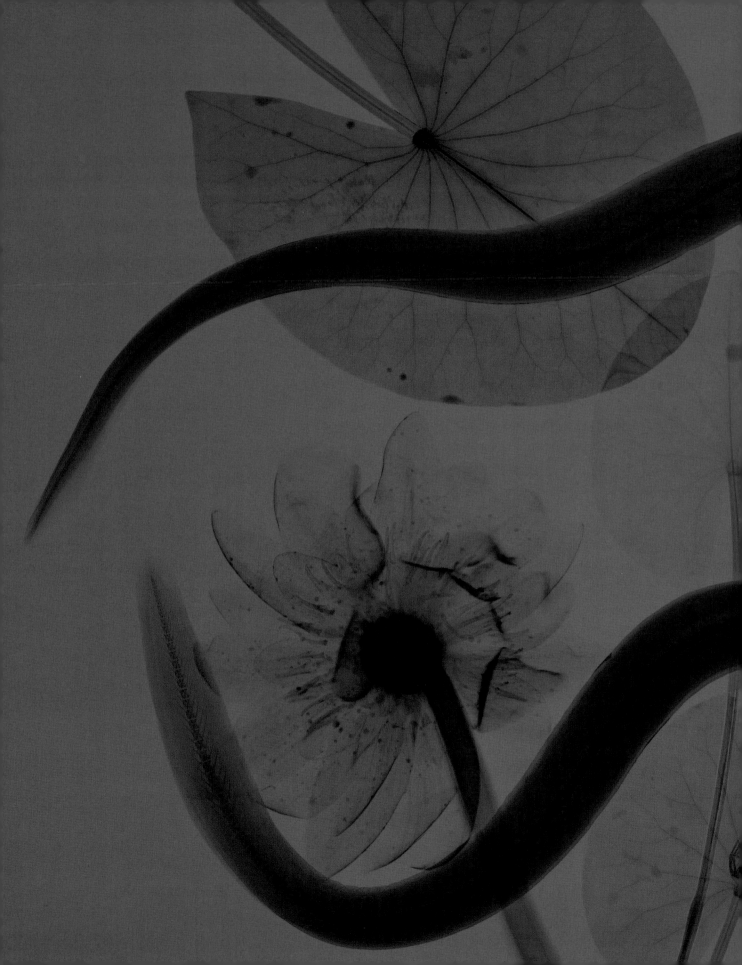

FISH

THE EEL

Swimming serpents

Eels are like snakes that swim. In the photo of the eels on the previous pages, you can make out two fins near the head, but if it weren't for their fins, these eels might easily be mistaken for cobras or boa constrictors. You can also see, in the eel at the top, that the eel's tail is thin and flat. This allows them to propel themselves forward in the water, so they don't have to rely on just those tiny fins to get around. They don't swim very quickly, but that's not a problem. Their food—mussels, fish eggs, larvae—usually stays still, so there's no need for them to be super-quick killers.

But then what is the advantage of having that long and twisted shape? Wouldn't it be handier just to have a few big fins? Well, eels live mostly at the bottom of rivers and lakes. Their narrow shape allows them to hide in cracks and crevices, so that they can look everywhere for food. They can also easily wrap themselves around reeds, water plants, and stones, or burrow into a layer of mud. That's useful when you need a place to hide quickly. If you're not fast, you need to be invisible.

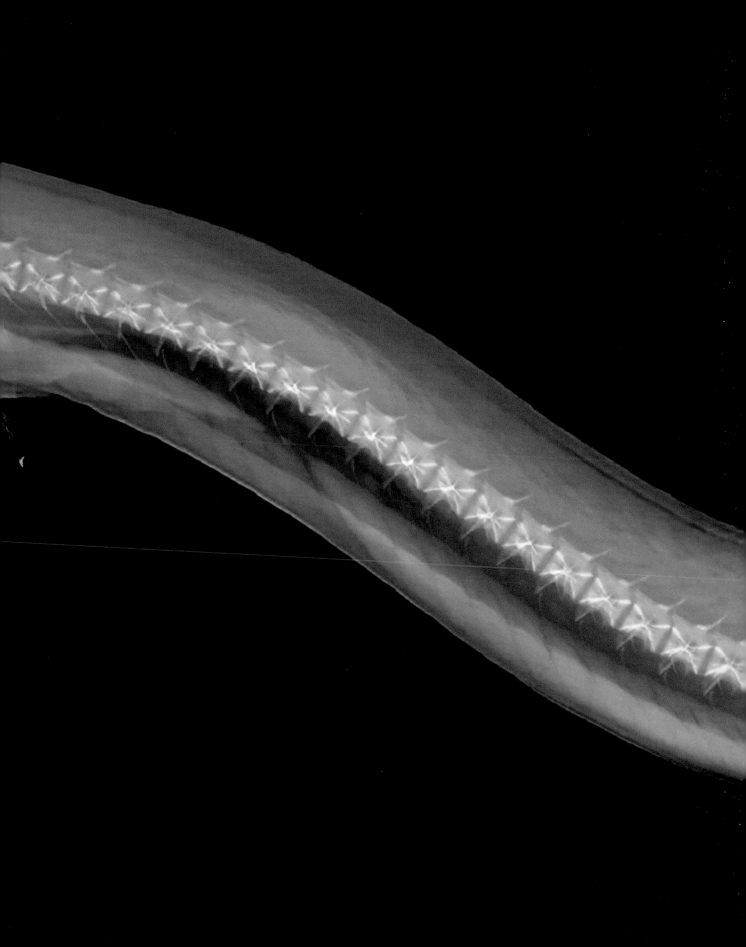

THE SILVER POMFRET

A bit of fish with your bones?

Insects, butterflies, snails: they have no use for bones. All bones do is add extra weight, and that's not something these animals want. It's a completely different story with humans though. Stand up. Go on! Now . . . imagine you didn't have any bones. How would you stay standing? If you managed it at all, it would take a huge effort. Or try lifting a heavy object with an outstretched arm. How would that work without bones? It'd be a lot more difficult, right? So now you see why you have bones.

But these silver pomfrets never have to stand upright. They just float around in the water. And fish don't have to shop at the grocery store either, so they don't need to carry anything heavy. Their skeleton still comes in handy though, because bones are important for lots of other things too. Bones give muscles something to hold on to. You can't shoot an arrow unless there's a bow attached to the string. And a slingshot that's nothing but a rubber band is no good, unless you make a frame with your fingers. But your fingers have bones too!

Bones also offer protection. This is true for all bone owners. You can see in the photograph exactly where the silver pomfret's bones are—they are the dark lines and patches. Where can you see the darkest patch in this silver pomfret? Just behind the eyes, where the brain is located. That's where you'll find the thickest bone. You can see this in every kind of fish. And the backbone, or spinal column, runs from the brain. That's where most of the nerves—the offshoots of the brain—are. These are very important, so they are well protected by a layer of bone. With every fish, all you have to do to follow its backbone to see where its brain is. In fish, that spinal column is fixed immovably to the skull. If a fish turns its body, its head automatically turns too.

It's tricky to eat a fish with so many bones though. So don't try ordering pomfret at a restaurant. You'd be much better off having "pommes frites" instead.

THE ROACH AND THE PERCH

Fishy failures

If you were to draw a fish without thinking too much about it, it would probably look basically like these two: the roach and the perch. In this photograph, you can barely tell them apart. But fish come in so many different shapes and sizes that almost every shape is possible—round or elongated, flat or spherical, smooth or with frills. Did you ever try to draw a fish and your drawing went wrong? Don't worry. There's probably a fish out there somewhere that's the spitting image of your attempt. Because there are so many fish and so many shapes. Although ... it's almost impossible to see the difference between the roach and the perch in this photograph.

In the photo, the fishes' swim bladders can clearly be seen though. They're those light patches under the spinal column. Swim bladders are bags that fish can inflate with gas, like a balloon. When the balloon is full, the fish rise in the water. When they want to sink, then they release gas from the bladder. By making themselves weigh the same as the water, they can ensure that they neither sink nor float to the surface.

The shape of a fish says a lot about its lifestyle. The shape of these roach and perch is one that is often seen in predators. These are not typical hunters, but they do eat small creatures, like insects. Their streamlined form helps them to shoot quickly through the water, which is also handy when they're being chased.

The fins belong to the skeleton too. They're important for moving forward and for staying upright. The back fins, for example, make sure that the fish doesn't roll upside down. The same goes for the fin underneath. Under the backbone, you can also see the pectoral fins; these are useful for steering and for braking. The tail fin in back is the main engine. One big swish of this fin and the fish shoots forward.

THE GARFISH
AND THE BARRACUDA
Sleek and speedy

There are hunters . . . and then there are hunters! You can tell by their shape that these barracudas on the right are as fast as an arrow. Can you see how long the swim bladder is? Such a long fish obviously needs a long swim bladder—otherwise the front would rise while the back sinks, or the other way around. But barracudas aren't just fast. They also rely on the element of surprise. They keep very still in the water, so that they're scarcely noticed. As soon as their prey comes by, they dart out.

The same is true of all fish with long, thin bodies, like the garfish below, for example. They're so beautifully streamlined that they look as if they are half fish, half harpoon. But to keep up their speed for a really long time, a fish, like a ship, needs a strong rudder: large, stiff tail fins. And even though the barracuda is speedy, it isn't the fastest fish, not by a long shot. The fastest fish are sailfish, tuna, and marlins. These fish have both a super-aerodynamic construction (in the water, it's actually called "hydrodynamic") *and* a powerful tail.

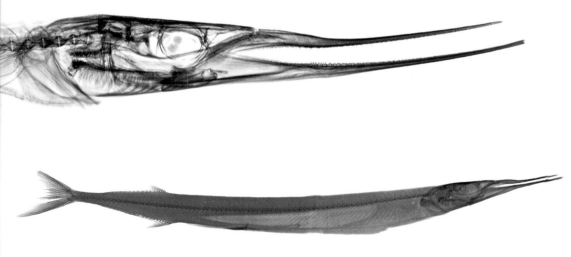

THE SMALL-SPOTTED CATSHARK

Just a big old pussycat!

The small-spotted catshark is less streamlined than some other fish, but it can make powerful strokes with its large fins. Its muscles are attached not only to its bones, but to its skin as well. That's because they have to be. Compare the bones of this catshark to those of other fish. It has none, except for the spinal column. Sharks are built in a completely different way than fish.

Unlike other fish, catsharks and other types of sharks don't have a swim bladder. Some sharks solve this problem by sucking in air, filling the space near their front fins, so that they can swim slowly without sinking. Other kinds of sharks have a different solution: they can produce oil in their livers. Oil is lighter than water, so it works just as well as air. And what about catsharks? They just sink to the bottom. They like it fine there. If they want to go up, then they swim.

The catshark isn't super-quick, but it can still swim much faster than you. Aaargh! Luckily, there's no need to be scared of them, because the catshark is harmless. It eats mainly shellfish, worms, and, very occasionally, small fish. Definitely no people. A great white shark would just laugh at the little catshark. Or gobble it up.

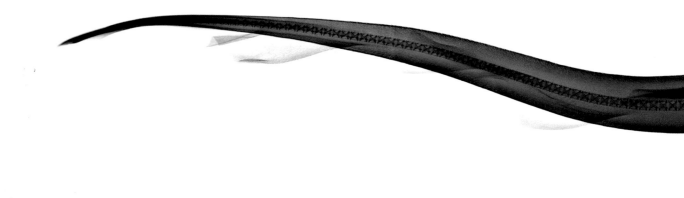

THE JOHN DORY

An underwater vacuum cleaner

When you're a predator, you don't necessarily need to be fast. The John Dory is more of a sneaky hunter. It carefully creeps up on its prey from behind. It helps that it is completely flat. As soon as it's right behind its victim, it strikes—not by darting after the prey, but by opening its mouth super-wide and super-fast. That way it sucks in the water, along with its prey, all in one go. It's a bit like using a vacuum cleaner to suck a fly off the wall: there is no escape.

Bigger fish do, of course, prey on the John Dory. That's how life goes in the sea. But the spikes on its back offer some protection. You might want to think twice before trying to swallow this fish whole.

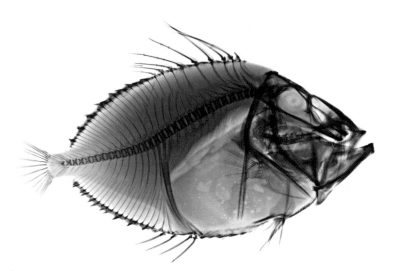

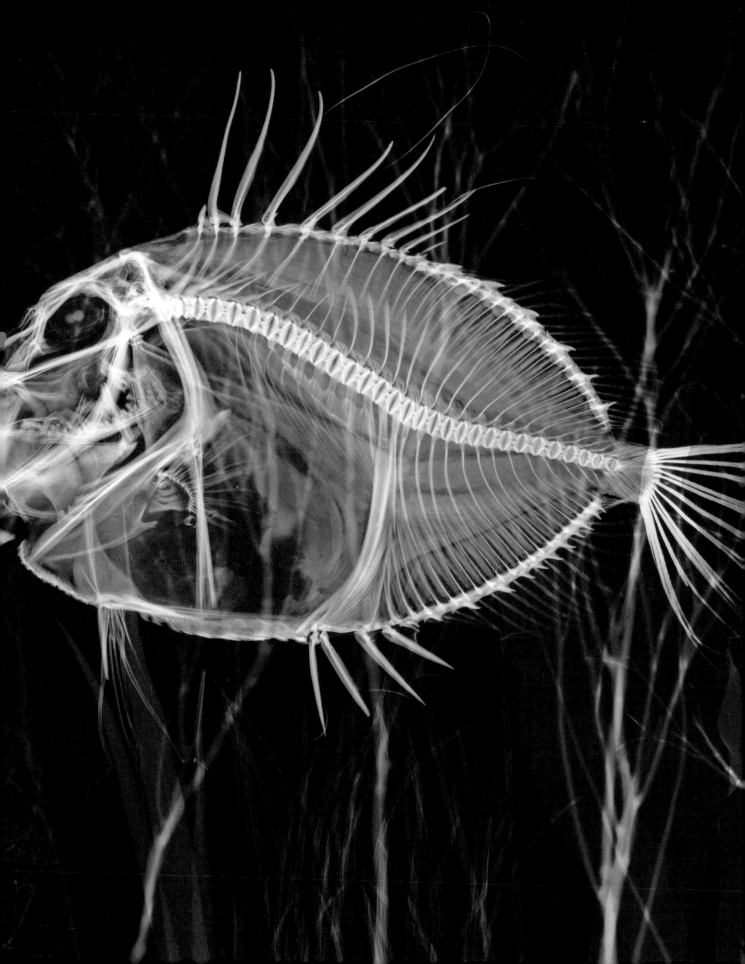

THE ANGLERFISH

Fish that go fishing

The anglerfish is another example of a fish that sucks in its prey, water and all. But it uses a very cunning trick to do so. It lives down at the bottom of the sea, and its camouflage makes it almost invisible. In this photograph of its mouth, you can see a small rod with a little blob on the end. If you're a fish, that blob looks like fish food. Small fish approach, but before they can take a bite, they get swallowed up. So human anglers aren't the only ones to use a fishing rod and bait. Nearly everything that humans have supposedly invented has actually been going on in nature for millions of years.

The anglerfish's backbone begins immediately behind its head. So you can clearly see how large this fish's head is compared to the rest of its body. It's also one of the few animals that has its eyes and its mouth on the top of its head. For us that would be really impractical, because we'd keep bumping into lampposts if we couldn't look ahead to see where we were going. For an anglerfish, though, it comes in handy, as it lives at the very bottom of the sea—where there are lantern fish, which produce light, but there aren't any lampposts at all.

THE CATFISH

Who are you calling a tongue?

Like the anglerfish, a catfish is also mostly made up of its head—and most of its head is its mouth. The size of that mouth is bad news for lots of other animals. Anything that is edible and fits inside the catfish's mouth can disappear into it: fish, birds, amphibians, and even some mammals!

The whiskers around its mouth are called barbels, and they work like feelers. However, this is not the catfish's only unusual ability. It can also sense electricity, which is useful because catfish feel most at home on the muddy bottoms of rivers and lakes, where it's impossible to see a fin in front of your face, so a built-in electricity meter comes in handy. That's because fish emit small electrical signals. The catfish can detect exactly where other fish are swimming and which way they're going.

The catfish's nose and ears work excellently too, as does its sense of taste. In fact, its sense of taste is particularly strong. We humans have taste buds only on our tongues, but the catfish has taste buds all over its body.

It's actually just one big swimming tongue—a tongue that works remotely. Fish secrete substances that flow with the water. A catfish tastes those substances and can then follow the taste. If it doesn't feel its prey electrically, doesn't smell it or see it, it can still taste it from a distance!

That's not all. Like most fish, catfish have another sense that we don't: the lateral line. This line cannot be seen in X-ray photos, but it runs from the fish's gills to its tail. With that lateral line, they can feel the smallest vibrations.

Eyes, ears, a nose, feelers, remote tasting, electro-sensors, and a lateral line: catfish are all about their senses. In oceans, great white sharks are the deadliest predators, but in lakes and rivers, it's catfish who deserve that title. A catfish was once found that was just over 9 feet (2.7 meters) long and weighed 646 pounds (293 kilograms). So it's just as well you don't fit into its mouth, or you might become its next victim.

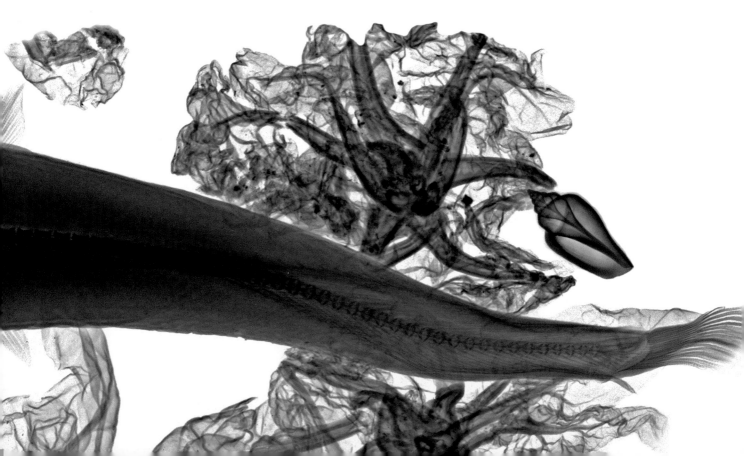

THE SOLE

Art and sole

The catfish might be covered with taste buds, but there's only one fish that can really be called a tongue. That's the sole. Huh? Well, in lots of languages, the name for the fishy sole is the same as the word for the tongue. In some other languages, including English, the fish got its name because it looked like a sandal, and so it became a sole, from the Latin word *solea*. A tongue, or a flat shoe? It looks a bit like both.

Lots of people agree that this fish is a delicious treat, so it's pretty expensive. What happens, though, if you run a restaurant and buy lots of expensive fish, but not many people order it? Then, pretty soon, the sole isn't too fresh anymore. Back in the 1960s, a sneaky chef came up with a solution for this problem: throw sweet fruit over it. Then no one can taste that the fish is going off. So take my advice and never order "sole Picasso."

That was what they called it, because the pieces of fruit make it look like a work of art by the famous painter.

In this photograph, are you looking at the fish from the side or from above? You might say from the side, but you'd be wrong. This animal has both eyes on the same side, so you're seeing it from above. It's as if you had two eyes on the left and none on the right. So, in a way, every sole is a sole Picasso, because that's how Picasso often painted both people and animals. The sole lives flat on the bottom of the sea, so an eye on its underside would be useless. It's much better off with two eyes on the top.

With lots of fish, their left and right sides are neat mirror images of each other. But this sole looks like a big old mess. It's a bag of bones! But the sole is actually very well constructed to suit the conditions it lives in. Tongue or sandal, it truly is a work of art.

THE RAY

Bend or break

Let's try a little experiment. Throw a rubber band onto the ground, as hard as you can. Now do the same with one of your parents' best vases. What happens? The rubber band will never break—and you can wave goodbye to your allowance for the next few months. Soft things cannot shatter, but hard things can. That's why you can easily break your bones, and this ray can't.

Rays, sharks, and a few other kinds of fish have bones made entirely out of cartilage. This makes their bones much softer and more flexible than ours. Cartilage *can* break, but you have to make quite an effort to do it. You have bits of cartilage here and there around your body too—in your nose, for instance, and in your ears, and between your joints. You can see it quite clearly in a chicken leg. It's that tough, rubbery tissue between the largest bones.

Just as an anglerfish is made up mostly of head, this thornback ray is made up mainly of fin. Its fins are more like wings, which it uses to fly through the water. These fins are all muscle, and thousands of small bones give the muscles something to hold on to.

You can also see the huge jaws, filled with rows of teeth. They're not sharp, pointed teeth though. They're flat, and therefore very useful for crushing and chewing. Rays make good use of their big jaws and grinding teeth, because they eat shellfish and crabs, complete with all the crunchy bits. And if one of their teeth falls out, the next one is already there, ready and waiting to come through.

Some rays also have a venomous tail that they can use to defend themselves, but this ray's tail is harmless. There are even aquariums where you can stroke these rays—that's how friendly they are. But do the rays enjoy it? If they were meant for cuddling, they'd be furry, wouldn't they?

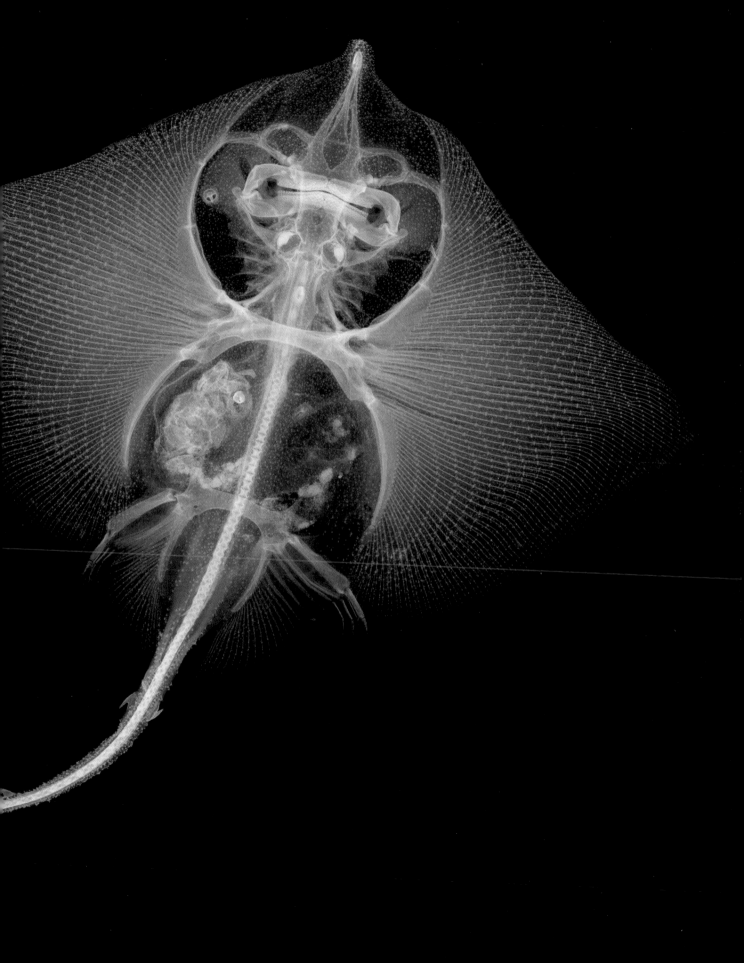

THE SEAHORSE

The odd fish out

Every kind of fish has its own shape, and each shape comes with its own advantages and disadvantages. Fish can be large, small, flat, long, short, round, prickly, smooth, with big fins or small fins—you name it. Have we described every possibility? No, the list goes on and on. What about the seahorse? Hmm, that's a tricky one. Even in a sea full of differences, the seahorse is the odd fish out.

For starters, the seahorse has a skeleton not only on the inside, but also on the outside. In this photograph, you can see lots of lumps and bumps. Together with tough plates, these form the seahorse's armor. After a predator has bashed its way through that armor, it then has to deal with the bones on the inside. All the dark places you can see in the X-ray are made of hard material. For most animals, that's way too much trouble to go to for such a small amount of fish. So they simply leave the seahorse alone.

Something else that makes it different? The seahorse has no stomach to store its food in! Whatever it eats goes straight to its gut. Also, the seahorse has a small, toothless snout that is unable to cope with large amounts of food. It also has a fused jaw, which means it has to suck its food in, as if through a straw. So the seahorse has to keep on eating all the time in order to absorb enough energy. It mostly eats little animals—lots and lots of little animals, all day long. So you might be as hungry as a horse, but being as hungry as a seahorse would be even worse.

And that's still not everything that makes the seahorse the odd fish out. Did you know that it's not the female seahorse that carries the eggs until the baby seahorses are ready to be born but the male? After the eggs have hatched, the pregnant male pushes little clouds of dozens of mini-seahorses out of his pouch. See, I said they were odd. Although... with an anteater's snout, a horse's head, an insect's shell, a fish's bones, a kangaroo's pouch, and a monkey's tail, maybe the seahorse isn't the odd one out at all. It's every animal, all at once!

AMPHIBIANS

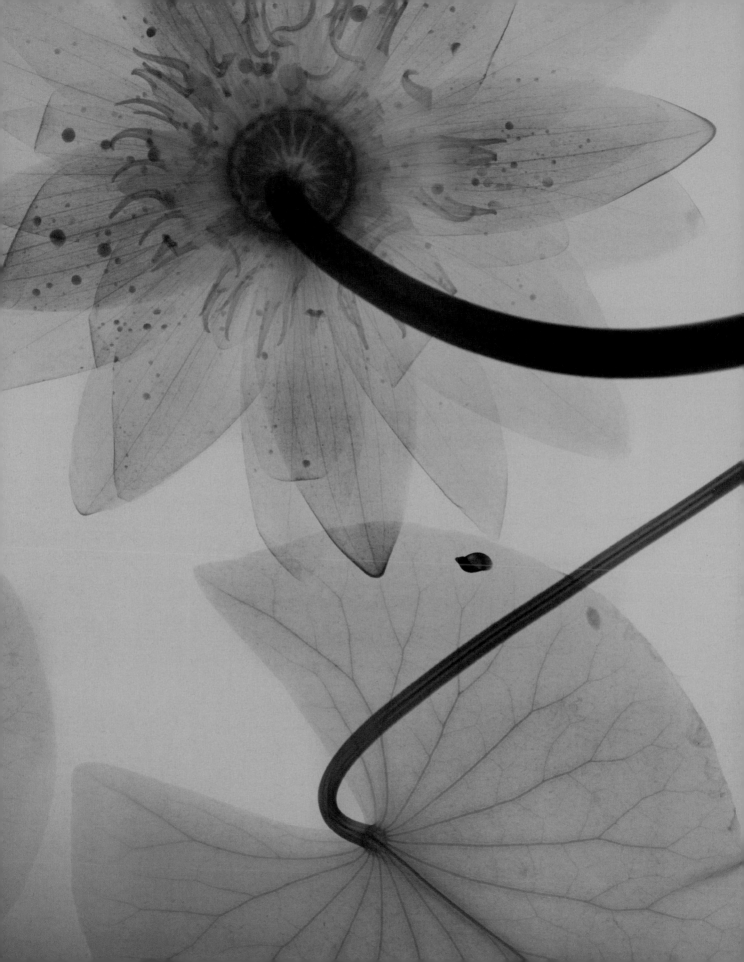

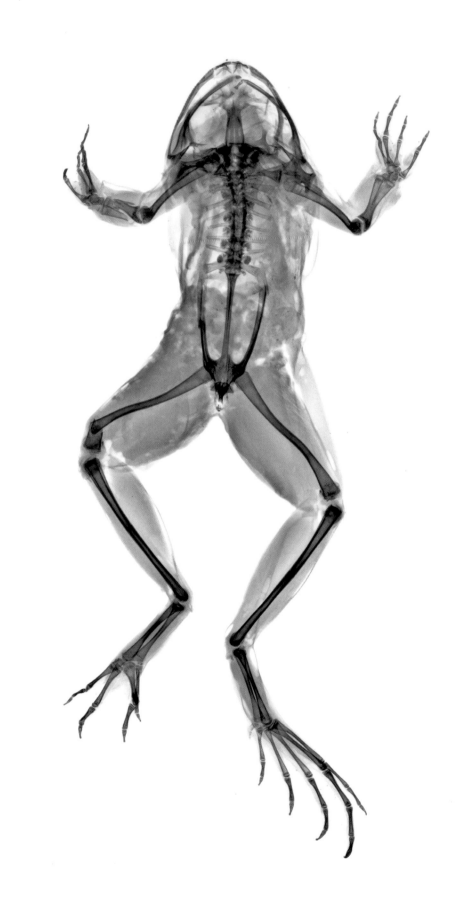

THE MARSH FROG

Why frogs are more skillful than princes

A frog turning into a prince? That could only happen in a fairy tale, right? But when you think about it, frogs have already been through a dramatic transformation once in their lives, so why shouldn't they be able to do it again? Frogs begin their lives as eggs and then tadpoles, which look like little fish. And then a minor miracle occurs. Halfway down their bodies, two back legs start to grow. Then two little front legs come along. The tail disappears, bit by bit, and the old tail parts are reused to make the rest of the frog, as if the animal were made out of tiny Lego bricks. Then it grows and grows and, before long, the frog is finished. The swimmer has transformed into a jumper.

A frog sitting on the ground is like a tightly wound spring. When it stretches its legs, it shoots forward like a cannonball. And the faster it stretches its legs, the farther it goes. The frog can do this because it has extra-long legs, including its upper legs, lower legs, and, um ... lower lower legs? Yes, that's what it looks like. Frogs have very long metatarsals, which are the bones in the middle of the foot. They're so long that it makes it seem as if the frog has an extra bit of leg. Just take a look. When a frog flies through the air, those legs, right to the tips of the toes, make one long, streamlined arch.

The rest of the frog's body is built for jumping too. Most frogs can jump about twenty times the length of their own body. If you could do that, you'd easily be able to jump over a school bus—the long way! And frogs are designed for safe landings, as well. They have extra-strong shoulder blades to absorb the impact on their front legs when they hit the ground. Instead of easily breakable ribs, they have sturdy protrusions on a very short backbone. Of course they need strong bones in their legs, and a special kind of pelvis, made up of two long, mobile bones with an extra bone in between for reinforcement. Their skeleton is light but still protective.

Frogs don't forget how to swim though. Like this European common brown frog in the photo on the right, most frog species still have handy webbed feet so they can move faster in the water. But instead of webs on their front feet they have four fingers that allow them to grasp. That's more useful on the land, particularly for frogs that like to climb trees.

These frogs are all perfectly constructed. They must be delighted that they won't really turn into princes. Because most princes are far less skillful than frogs.

THE TREE FROG
Eating with your eyes

In the photo on the right, you can clearly see every bone in this tree frog's body. You'll notice how big its eyes are in comparison to the rest of its head. They bulge outward, like a gun turret on a bunker. That allows the frog to look forward, backward, and all the way to the side. You can also see its teeth around the edge of its head. Most frogs have teeth only in their upper jaws, although there is one species that also has teeth in its lower jaw. A frog's tongue doesn't begin in its throat, as it does in humans, but halfway into its mouth. That allows the frog to stick the tongue out extra far and to snatch insects lickety-split. But is that really a big advantage?

Imagine if your tongue were only at the front of your mouth...and now take an imaginary bite of a sandwich. How would you get the sandwich down into your throat? You wouldn't. It's impossible. But that's where the frog's huge eyes come in handy. To move the food in its mouth backward, the frog squeezes its eyes shut. The eyes then push the food into its throat. So sometimes there are advantages to having eyes bigger than your stomach.

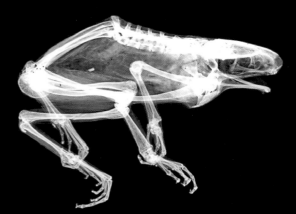

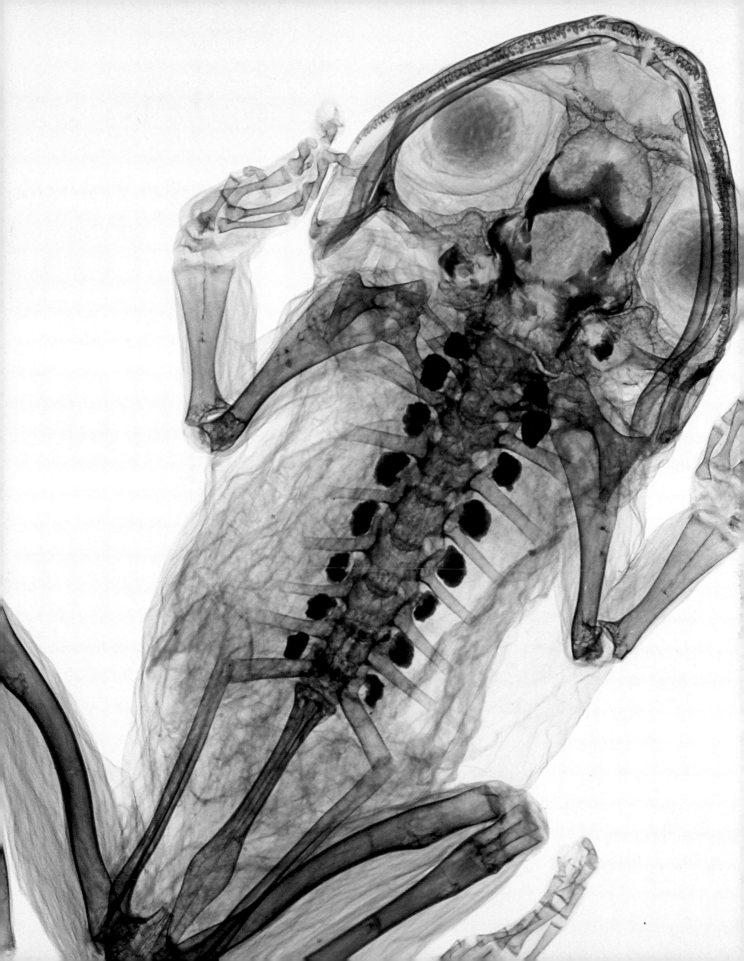

REPTILES

It's about time we put a dinosaur into the X-ray machine. I mean, that's obviously what we're dealing with here, right? You can see that just by looking at it. Too bad it's not standing on its hind legs, because then you could see even more clearly that this is a cousin of the *Tyrannosaurus rex*. But hang on a moment. Aren't its legs a bit short for a *T. rex*? And didn't dinosaurs die out long ago? Hmm, then it must be a lizard, not a dinosaur. It's still a "saur" though, because that part of the word "dinosaur" comes from *sauros*, the Greek word meaning lizard. Lizards lived alongside the dinosaurs for years. Once upon a time, they were neighbors.

This tegu doesn't only resemble a dinosaur. It's also a bit like us humans. Look at it: a big skull covering the brain, ribs to protect the lungs and the heart, one upper leg bone and two lower leg bones, followed by a few smaller carpal bones, and then the five fingers and toes. Just like us.

By counting the fingers, you can tell if an animal is an amphibian or a reptile: amphibians have only four fingers, while reptiles have five. If you look closely at the teeth, you'll see that it has pointed teeth at the front. You can compare these to a predator's fangs. At the back, it has the teeth of a herbivore, a plant-eater. So the tegu is an omnivore, like us, which means that it eats everything.

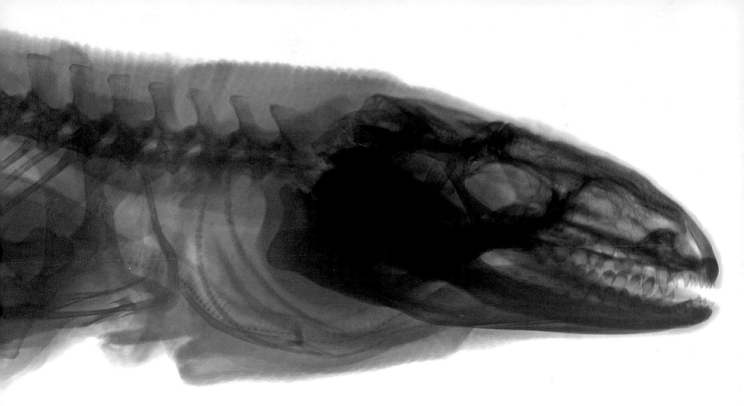

That huge tail, though, really belongs to lizards alone. Even dogs, kangaroos, and tigers wish they could have a super-tail like that. And tegus and most other lizards can lose their tails on command. For example, if they're threatened by a predator, three-quarters of their tail falls off and goes on wriggling for a bit. While the attacker is still staring in amazement, the tegu makes its escape. But without its tail.

That's not a disaster though, as the tail grows back again. If your arm gets pulled off, you obviously won't grow a new one, but that's exactly what happens with the tegu's tail. The new tail isn't quite as fine as the old one though. Instead of the strong vertebrae the old tail had, the new one is built with just a soft rod of cartilage. And Tail 2.0 is a bit smaller and less flexible too. But otherwise it's great. All fixed and—almost—as good as new.

The new tail doesn't appear overnight though. It needs time to grow. And life can be pretty tricky for a lizard without a tail. Lizards use their tails to communicate, to store energy, and to help them keep their balance. So a lizard is never going to abandon its tail just for the fun of it. When it's a question of life and death, however, they don't think too long about it: the tail has to go. And it's a method that works. Because dinosaurs became extinct millions of years ago, but lizards are still around.

THE BEARDED DRAGON
A spiny beard

Water can be a real lifesaver if you're dying of thirst. But it's also your best friend when you're jumping off the highest diving board: the water absorbs a lot of the impact when you hit. That relatively soft landing is why strong bones are less important in water than on land, and why land animals benefit more from having strong bones.

You can't be much more of a land animal than the bearded dragon, because it lives in the driest environment on Earth—in the desert. You can see how its ribs protect its entire belly and chest. The only spot that's not encased by bones is between its front paws and lower jaw, but that's where its most important defense is located: its "beard." If it meets an enemy, it puffs up its beard to make a big shield of scary spines. You can see in the photograph how it does that. Under its jaw, there are curved bones. The bearded dragon puts these up like a tent, so that its beard is suddenly very big. That's often all it takes to scare off an enemy, which is just as well, because bearded dragons can't lose their tails as a defensive tactic—even though they're lizards.

You see that the back legs are larger and more powerful than the front legs. When they're in danger, lizards sprint away with those strong back legs. They can go incredibly fast. Some lizards, like the plumed basilisk, can go so fast that they can actually run on water. That's how the plumed basilisk got its other name, the Jesus Christ lizard. The bearded dragon can't do that trick, but if its spiny beard doesn't help, it can still make a very quick getaway.

THE LONG-TAILED GRASS LIZARD

Snakes with legs

Look at the two lizards in the photograph on the left. Can you follow their bodies all the way to the end of their tails? Tricky, huh? The tail of a long-tailed grass lizard can be up to five times longer than its body. Is that useful? Well, imagine you want to jump into the air and you have that big, long tail trailing after you. Not so easy. Or if you want to sprint away. Your long tail won't be much help then either.

Long-tailed grass lizards are small creatures and very, very light. Their tails weigh so little that they can easily climb up tall stalks of grass, where there's more sunlight to warm them up and they can see from a height if there's danger nearby. They even jump from stalk to stalk, and the tail comes in handy then because it helps them to keep their balance.

How else does the tail help? Long-tailed grass lizards are sometimes called snakes with legs, because, when you see them slithering through the grass, their legs are totally invisible. Then they're almost impossible to tell apart from snakes. And many of the lizard's predators want to steer clear of snakes, even little ones. Sadly, not every animal is fooled by those sneaky snake tails. And some predators quite like the idea of a snake as a snack. So they still go after these lizards. But can you guess what trick the lizard has to fall back on? That's right: when danger approaches, it's off with the tail—and scoot!

THE MONITOR LIZARD AND THE PYTHON

A legless lizard

If a long-tailed lizard is a snake with legs, then this python could just as easily be called a lizard without legs—you can see how much the skeletons of this monitor lizard and the python resemble each other. Lizards and snakes—they're all part of the same big family.

Monitor lizards and pythons are both predators and partly share the same menu: rodents, lizards, birds, amphibians. But pythons also sometimes eat larger mammals when they get the chance, while monitor lizards eat smaller creatures, such as insects and spiders. Monitor lizards and pythons also live in more or less the same areas. They both have forked tongues that they use for smelling, too.

Those legs are obviously an important difference though. The distant ancestors of snakes did have legs. But they used those legs less and less over the course of thousands and thousands of years, until the legs eventually disappeared. For tens of millions of years, they've coped just fine without legs. Pythons can strangle their prey by winding tightly around them. Monitor lizards can grasp their prey with their legs. But actually that's rarely necessary: both usually strike in a flash, with their prey dead and in their mouths in an instant. Why make the job difficult when you can do it super-fast?

THE CROCODILE AND THE PYTHON

A couple of losers

A crocodile and a python. Put them together, and you've got a whole load of deadly, razor-sharp teeth. Which of the two would win in a fight? On the internet, you can find lots of gruesome videos of fights between crocodiles and snakes. Sometimes the snake wins; sometimes the croc.

These are both creatures that rely on surprise attacks. The python in the photo would seem to have the sneaky advantage. But the python is a constrictor, not a venomous snake, so it has to be capable of squeezing all the air out of that crocodile, bit by bit. Bear in mind, though, that the crocodile can go without air for a very long time. The crocodile is also much bigger and stronger. In the picture on the right, you can see that its front leg doesn't start until that dark patch to the right of the vertebrae. And in the background of the photo, you can make out the rest of its big body. Hmm . . . who's going to win?

Of course, in this photo the confrontation is staged. The crocodile and the python are as dead as dodos. So, in fact, they've both already lost.

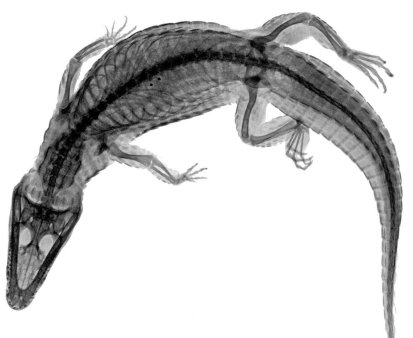

THE CHAMELEON
The tongue of death

Whenever you hear something about chameleons, it's nearly always about their skin. As everyone knows, a chameleon's skin can change color. But that's not really all that special when you think about it. When humans find out that their zipper has been down for hours, they suddenly change color too. An X-ray can't show the chameleon's colors, so now we have a good opportunity to talk about more interesting things for once.

For example, look at the chameleon's tail, which curls so beautifully, like a young fern leaf. The tail is hugely strong, and when the chameleon climbs a tree it uses it like a fifth leg. And what about those legs, with toes like a tow truck's hook that can grip branches? Like an owl, the chameleon has toes that spread out nicely on both sides of its feet. But none of that is anywhere close to the most remarkable thing about this animal. What is most amazing about the chameleon is its tongue.

The tongue is the chameleon's most important weapon. It can pick its prey out of a tree at a speed of 80 feet per second (25 meters per second). Have you ever seen one of those popguns that shoot a cork attached to a string? The chameleon's tongue is a bit like that. There's no cork on the end, but a sticky pad that grabs its victim.

A chameleon's tongue can be twice as long as its body (without the tail). That enormous tongue is folded up inside its little head like an accordion. It only fits because it's kind of like a rubber band, so it's a lot shorter when it's not being stretched. Inside the chameleon's mouth there is also a tongue bone that works like the Y-shaped frame of a slingshot. Using that frame and the powerful muscles in its mouth, the chameleon shoots out its rubber-band tongue at a huge speed. So the chameleon's tongue is very handy indeed. But there's something we can do with our tongue that chameleons can't. We can talk. The chameleon uses its colored skin to communicate instead.

THE RED-EARED SLIDER TURTLE
Cold-blooded centenarians

Like seahorses, turtles have double protection, from inside and out, with both a shell and bones. You can see that clearly in the photos on the left. You can tell that the shell is not very thick though, because you can see the legs and all the other bones. However, the shell does not need to be very thick, because the red-eared slider turtle lives mainly in the water. This seems to be working out pretty well, as turtles can live to a very old age.

These red-eared slider turtles "only" live to around 50 years old. That's quite something for such a small animal, because small animals don't generally live as long as bigger ones. Giant tortoises, which are also a kind of turtle, live even longer. The oldest one ever was called Adwaita, and he might have been as old as 250 when he died in 2006. The oldest tortoise whose age we know fairly precisely is Tu'i Malila, who definitely reached the age of somewhere between 189 and 193.

So it's handy to be well protected. But that's not the turtle's real secret for reaching a ripe old age. The secret is their metabolism. Turtles have an incredibly slow metabolism. That means they use little energy. The slower your metabolism, the longer your cells last. And the longer your cells last, the longer you can live. The oldest animal ever wasn't a turtle—it was a clam that made it to no less than 507 years old. Shellfish are known to be able to bring their metabolism almost to a stop. That's impossible for humans. It would mean we couldn't heat our bodies to 98.6 degrees Fahrenheit (37 degrees Celsius).

Humans and other mammals are warm-blooded. We burn energy in our bodies to warm ourselves. Like other reptiles, turtles are cold-blooded. They don't heat themselves up—they use the warmth of the sun instead. The shell of this red-eared slider turtle is not just a shield. It's also a solar panel. So, in the warm sunshine, the turtle has more energy and moves more quickly than it does in the cool water.

If you want to live to be a couple of hundred years old, you'll have to wear a helmet and a shield—and also find out how to transform from a warm-blooded animal into a cold-blooded one.

THE CONSTRICTOR
The bigger the appetite, the bigger the mouth

Three guesses what a rat snake eats. Exactly! Mice! And frogs, birds, lizards, and—oh, yes!—rats. Nothing unusual about that, you might think. Until you realize that the head of the rat snake (right) is much smaller than your fist, and that a rat is much bigger than that. A rat snake is a constrictor, so we know it strangles its prey rather than poisoning it. But how can a small snake get a whole rat into its stomach without the help of a knife and fork? The answer to this puzzle is in the snake's skull. This has a very handy design—not just in constrictors but in all snakes.

Hold your hand in the shape of a snake's head, like the python's head on the left. Your thumb is the lower jaw, and your fingers form the upper jaw. Now open the "mouth" of the "snake" as wide as possible. That's how wide the real snake can open its mouth too, so a big animal will fit inside. The jaws of a snake aren't attached to anything. And the left and right lower jaws are separate, so that the mouth can open wider sideways to let more in as well. The snake's backward-pointing teeth push the prey deeper into the throat with every bite.

A snake's throat and stomach are extremely elastic, so that everything that goes in through the mouth can easily slip on down. The rib cage also bends apart to make more room. Some larger snakes can manage to down an entire goat. That does look pretty weird though: a thin snake with a huge bulge in the middle. Like you've just vacuumed up a soccer ball and it's stuck halfway down the hose. The prey is digested in the stomach over the course of a few days, unless the prey is especially big. Eventually, all that's left of the victim is a few small pieces of poop. The rest simply disappears, from head to tail.

Speaking of tails . . . do snakes actually *have* a tail? Or *are* they a tail? Before you start racking your brain, we already have the answer for you: snakes *do* have a tail. The cloaca—the hole they use for pooping, peeing, and laying eggs—is not at the end of the snake, but some way before that. The part that comes after the cloaca is the tail. And it's a useful tail too. A snake can wiggle its tail a little bit so that it looks like a worm. Other animals approach to get the worm—and the snake grabs them! So, you could say that even non-venomous snakes have a stinger in their tail.

BIRDS

THE BARN OWL

Big guy, huh?

When we see a bird, we *think* we're seeing a bird. In reality, we're just seeing a whole bunch of feathers on legs. The real bird is hidden somewhere deep inside those feathers. The photo (right) of two owls shows what these birds are really made of. That impressive barn owl below turns out to be just a scrawny little owlet without its down jacket. Hmm, "little"? The barn owl can grow to over 15 inches (40 centimeters), and it catches all kinds of rodents and small birds with the greatest of ease. And I don't imagine it would be nice to feel those pointed claws jabbing the back of your neck—not to mention that razor-sharp beak.

And don't forget that the birds that the owl catches are hidden under a load of feathers too, so most of them are way smaller than this "little" owl. In short, it's not all about being big. What matters is being bigger.

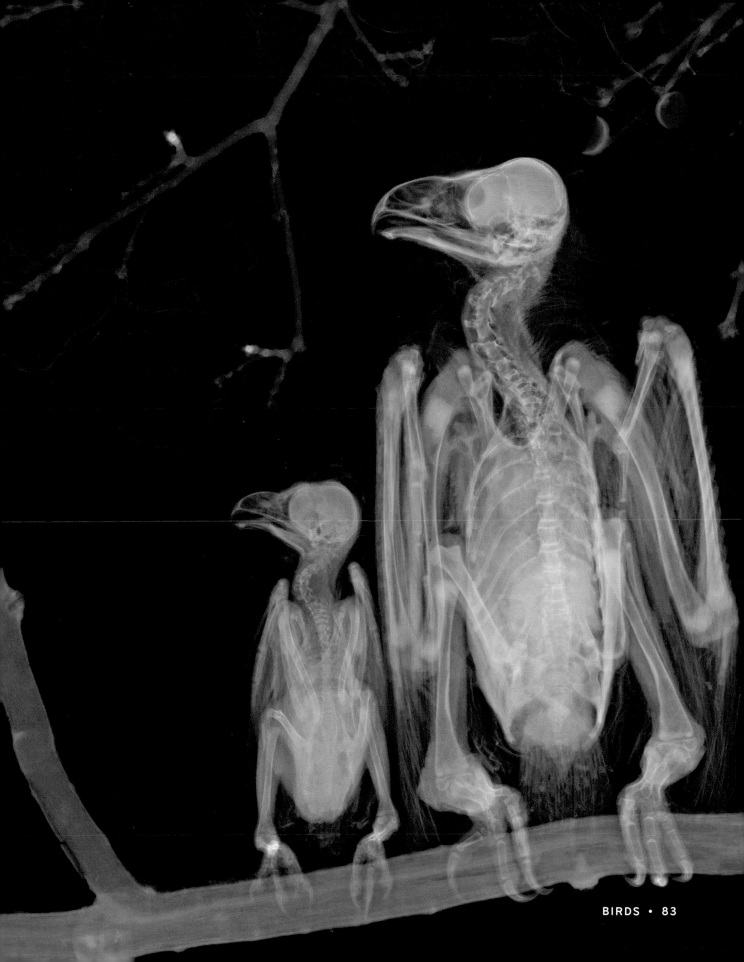

THE WAGTAIL

Swimming in the air

Birds are often beautiful to look at, and even the less beautiful ones can be amazing whistlers. Everyone knows that. But not a lot of people know that birds are at least as special on the inside. For centuries, our ancestors tried everything in their power to fly like birds. They never succeeded. And why not? Because they always looked at the outside of birds and not at the inside. That was foolish. If they'd looked more closely at the birds' skeletons, they'd have known that it's completely impossible for humans to flap themselves up into the air with a pair of homemade wings on their arms.

If you want to fly, you have to be light, and you need to have a lot of air resistance. That's why it's easier to blow a feather up above your head than a rock. For birds, air resistance is created by their outspread wings, which they use to push themselves up into the sky. It's as if they're swimming the butterfly stroke on the wind. But you can only do that if you're very light *and* very strong. Which birds are—and we are not.

Now, if you look at this photo of a wagtail, you can see a lot of bones. And bones are heavy, aren't they? Nope. At least, not if you're a bird. The bones in this wagtail are practically hollow, like drinking straws, and they weigh barely anything. It's as though they contain lots of little air bubbles. That makes the bird's bones both strong and light. Even its beak is light. It's not made of bone. It's made of keratin, the same stuff your hair is made of. Nice and light!

In the photograph, you can also see where birds get their strength from. On the front of the wagtail, you can see a big light patch running from the bottom of the belly to the top of the chest. That's the keel bone. Humans have a breastbone there, which is relatively small, but in birds this bone is gigantic. It has to be, because the bone needs to support the huge cluster of muscles that birds need in order to be able to fly. As far as muscles are concerned, no bodybuilder in the world comes anywhere close to the muscles that this wagtail has in its chest. And without those muscles, you won't get into the air, particularly if you have heavy human bones.

THE LONG-EARED OWL
Back-to-front knees

Something's not quite right here. The long-eared owl on the right has its knees pointing toward us, and it is looking to the side. At least that's what it looks like. But if that's true, then its legs are pointing in the wrong direction. Don't animals' knees bend backward? And if it were standing with its back toward us, then its knees would be on the wrong side! Hmm. But wait a minute . . . are those really knees? Do long-eared owls actually have knees?

Yes, owls do have knees. And those knees face the same way as human knees. They're just hard to see. With the buzzard below, you can see far more clearly how it works. When we say that animals' knees bend backward, what we're really looking at is not their knees at all. What looks like the upper leg of the long-eared owl is not an upper leg, but a lower leg, which makes those "knees" ankles. What looks like its lower leg is the metatarsal, to which its toes are attached. And its upper leg is hidden under its feathers. So they have the same bones as we do, pointing the same way.

Phew. I'm glad we got that straight.

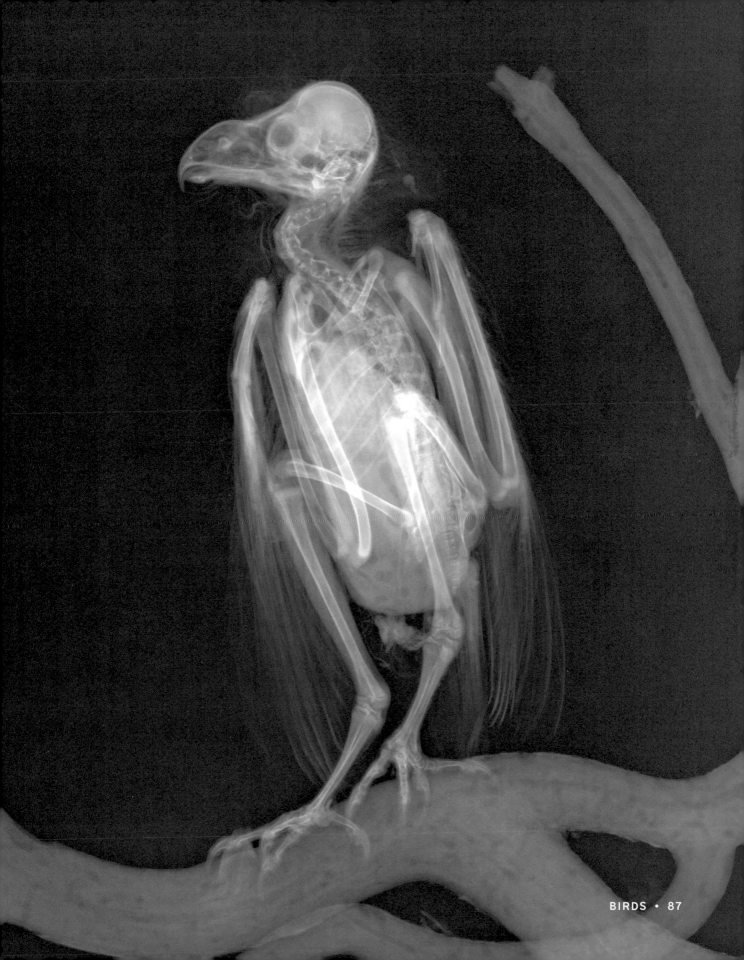

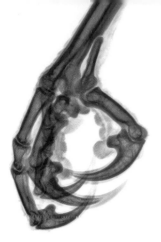

THE BUZZARD
Out of hand

You can see clearly from this buzzard that the "arms" of a bird are quite a lot like ours, but with some important differences. As with humans, the upper arm bone (humerus) runs into the two lower arm bones (the radius and the ulna). But then it gets kind of out of hand. The buzzard's metacarpals (the bones in the middle of the "hand") are long, while its "fingers" are short. It's exactly the other way around with humans. Buzzards do have a thumb like us, which you can see at the top. There are extra feathers attached to it, so that they can use it to steer.

The dark patch under the upper arm bones shows the bunch of muscles that the bird has there. There are far fewer muscles around the actual wing bones. Birds fly mainly with their chest muscles and much less with their "arm muscles."

There's another dark patch, and it's in the bird's throat. In the X-ray photo below, you can see what's causing it: it's swallowing a mouse!

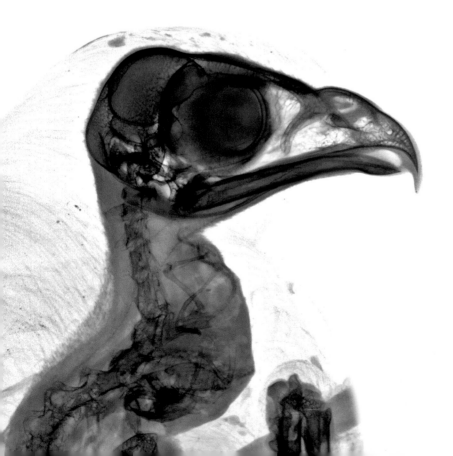

THE PHEASANT

Mini-ostriches

Birds like swifts stay in the air almost their entire lives. They live there, eat there, and sleep there (although we don't know exactly how). But pheasants feel more at home on the ground. When there's danger, they actually try to run away first. But if that doesn't work, they give flying a try. In the X-ray photo below, you can see why: pheasants are pretty heavy birds with quite bulky tails. They also like to eat seeds, tubers, grass, and fruit, which you find on the ground and not in the air.

So strong legs are no use to swifts, but they're certainly important to pheasants. Pheasants have sturdy upper and lower legs, but those heavy legs give them much more weight to carry when flying. And the heavier the legs are, the harder it is to fly, so the more they prefer to walk—and that makes their legs even more muscular. If this continues then in thousands of years pheasants might have huge legs, just like ostriches! Or if the pheasant encounters a new land predator, maybe it will need to start flying more, and then its legs will become smaller?

For now, pheasants are comfortable with their bodies. They can easily reach speeds of around 35 miles per hour (60 kilometers per hour) and also strut long distances across the fields. And do you see that sharp point at the back of the foot? That's a spur, a very handy and dangerous weapon with which it can seriously injure its enemies. So, maybe pheasants will stay just as they are for a while longer.

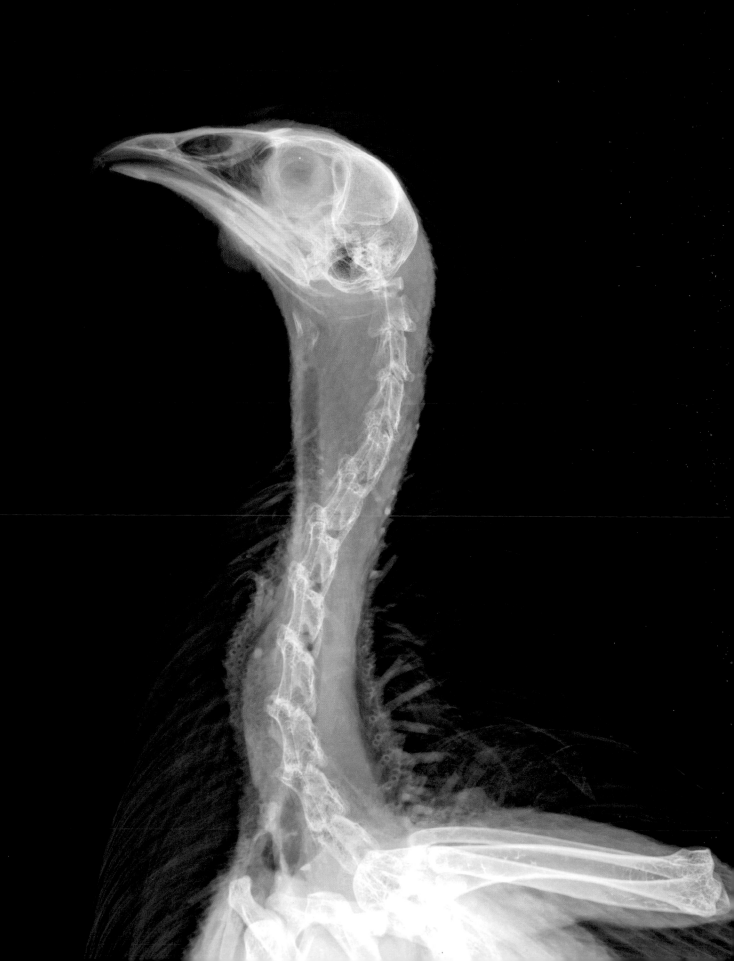

THE JAY

Sleeping on one leg

For flightless birds, or birds that spend a lot of time running, like the pheasant, big, strong legs are very useful. Other birds may have scrawny little legs, but they can still do remarkable things. Birds have sturdy claws that they can clasp tightly around branches. Some birds even prefer to sleep on one leg, snuggling the other leg up against themselves, nice and warm. Gripping the branch is no effort for them, even when they're asleep, because the bird's weight causes a tendon to pull the claws together in a tight grip. So standing firmly on one leg is a cinch.

We humans are made up very differently indeed. Or would you like to try sleeping high up in a treetop on one leg too?

THE DUCK

Land-air-and-water birds

Some birds feel more at home in the air, some prefer to be on the ground, and others are as happy as a fish in the water. As with land-based birds, the legs of water birds immediately reveal where they like to hang out—after all, webbed feet aren't much use in a tree.

A duck's webbed feet work better than those rubber flippers you can buy in diving stores. As soon as ducks move their feet forward through the water, the webs fold in two so that they can glide smoothly with little resistance. When they push their feet back, the webs open up again, so that they have extra pushing power in the water. That's how ducks propel themselves forward.

A duck's beak is all about the water too. It's actually like a sieve, because it has lots of little slits around the edges. When they are underwater, ducks let their beaks fill up. Then they push out the water with their tongues and eat all the water plants and animals left behind in the "sieve." And thanks to their long necks, they can easily reach into all kinds of places.

Imagine being able to walk *and* fly *and* spend all day bobbing around in ponds and streams. Ducks have got it made. It's actually not fair to call them water birds. They are, of course, land-air-and-water birds.

MAMMALS

THE BAT
Flap your hands

You don't need to be a bird or an insect to be able to fly. Mammals can do it too, as long as they have very big hands. Hands? Yes, just take a look. The wings of a bat extend along its arm bones, the same as a bird's, but mostly they surround the bat's hands. Bats have extremely long fingers. Only their thumbs are small—those are the tiny bits sticking out from the top of the wings. Bats don't have handy feathers like a bird. They just use their skin to fly. And bats don't have bones filled with air pockets the way birds do, so bats have very thin bones instead to keep them as light as possible.

Bats' back legs are pretty small compared to the rest of their bodies. They can barely sit on those legs, if at all. So they don't bother. They prefer to hang, and their claws are made in such a way that they can sleep while hanging. Once bats are hanging, their claws "lock," like birds' feet, and do not let go.

It's hard to see this in the X-ray photo, but bats' knees turn exactly the opposite way to ours or dogs' or cats'. When a bat crawls across the ground, its knees stick upward, which makes it look pretty clumsy—it doesn't help that its front legs are covered in wings. But thanks to its claws the bat can just as easily crawl upside down across the ceiling of a cave, and then it looks pretty cool.

With its mammal skeleton, the bat looks much more human than all the animals we've seen so far. Its skeleton is even more like a human's skeleton than it is like a mouse's. So maybe we should start calling them "bat people" from now on. But wait a second. Isn't there already someone like that? In Gotham City?

THE MOUSE
Super-mice

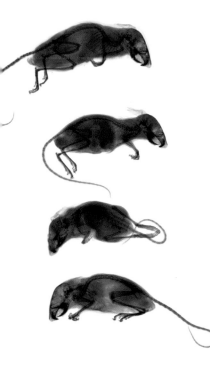

Thanks to their clever bodies, mice can do almost anything they want to. You could almost be jealous of them. Their bones are thin and light, but very strong. And those bones are surrounded by supple muscles that are very powerful. Mice can use them for climbing, running, jumping, crawling, digging, and swimming. Their hugely strong back legs allow them to get up onto your kitchen counter or into your cabinets with ease. Using the paws and claws on their front legs, they can grip almost anything. Mice can't quite manage to fly, but otherwise they're real all-rounders—and apparently they're omnivores too, eating everything.

Every day they head out to find food up to twenty times. Seeds, fruit, small animals: they nibble up whatever is edible. Those razor-sharp little teeth are a big help, of course. They cut through the hardest nuts, the thickest roots, and the toughest power cables. What? They eat power cables too? No, but they do give them a good chew. They'll also munch on insulation material, books, and old junk in attics and basements—they gnaw them all up to use as construction material for their nests. So maybe they're not actually omnivores, but they're certainly omni-gnawers.

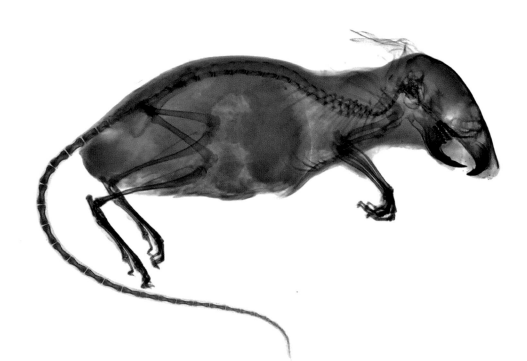

THE RAT
Family feud

It's easy to see that mice and rats are family. At first sight, this rat looks like an overgrown mouse. It's hard to tell the difference between a young rat and an adult mouse in an X-ray photo. But there are a few differences. The head of the rat is a bit more sturdy. Its legs are a little bigger, while its ears are a little smaller. Finally, its tail is slightly thicker. You can easily tell the difference by their poop though: rat droppings are a lot bigger than mouse droppings.

The most important difference can be seen in their behavior: rats hunt mice, but mice do not hunt rats. Mice are terrified of rats, in fact. Just the smell of a rat is enough to send shivers down a mouse's spine. So if you want to get rid of a mouse, you're better off scaring it away with the smell of a rat than tempting it with a chunk of cheese. There's no doubt about it—rats and mice can't stand each other. But hey, what family doesn't fight now and then?

THE SHREW AND THE VOLE

A case of mistaken identity

A bat might look like a winged mouse, but it clearly is *not* a mouse. And this vole (right) isn't a mouse either, in spite of the close resemblance. It is, of course, a rodent, like a rat or a mouse. But the vole is more closely related to a hamster. If you want to tell the difference between these animals, just look at their teeth. There are other animals that look a lot like mice but are actually something else, like the shrew, for example. Shrews belong to the mole and hedgehog family.

No matter how much shrews and voles might look like mice, they belong to completely different species. Mice, voles, and shrews actually look more similar than some breeds of dogs. What about a tiny Chihuahua and a great big Saint Bernard? They don't look much like each other, do they? But they're still the same species. Confusing, huh?

Dogs, cats, and mice are clearly three different species. But Chihuahuas, Saint Bernards, and dachshunds are separate breeds within one species: the dog. So the difference between breeds and species is not in their appearance. You belong to the same species if you can reproduce with another animal of the same kind and produce healthy babies that are also able to reproduce. So a Chihuahua and a Saint Bernard could make a family, but a dog and a cat can't. If you tried to cross them, you wouldn't get any babies. And when animals of two different species do somehow succeed in breeding, then their children are infertile. There are, for example, animals known as ligers and tigons, which are crosses between tigers and lions, and they're unable to have cubs.

On the left of the picture, you can see a weasel, by the way. It looks a lot like a stoat. How do you tell them apart? No problem. A weasel is weasily recognized—and a stoat is stotally different!

THE RABBIT AND THE HARE
Same but different

Hmm. More animals that look like each other! Nature's rule: if something works, don't change it. That seems to apply to the skeletons of small mammals. But there are a few differences here, of course. Hares are usually a bit bigger and stronger, with longer ears and, in particular, larger hind legs.

However, it's still mainly the similarities that you notice. With both hares (right) and rabbits (below), the back legs are much bigger than the front legs. That's what gives them their speed and jumping power. Their front legs function mainly as landing gear after every jump. The teeth are also very similar. They're very long and start growing deep inside the jaw. At the front, you can see a double set of razor-sharp incisors and at the back are the molars. Another striking feature of both animals is that they have pretty thin bones in places where there's a large muscle mass. This allows them to run fast, but it also means they're more likely to break a bone on the way.

Animals that look so much like each other will probably behave like each other too, right? Well, not really. Hares live alone, and rabbits live in groups. Hares sleep outside in a hollow, and rabbits sleep in a burrow underground. Newborn hares are ready to go, but rabbits are born bald, blind, and helpless. Hares are also stronger and can run longer and faster. So if they had a race, the hare would win by more than, ahem, a hair.

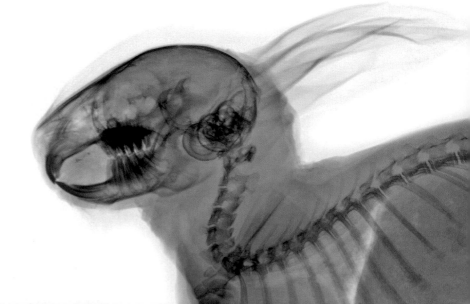

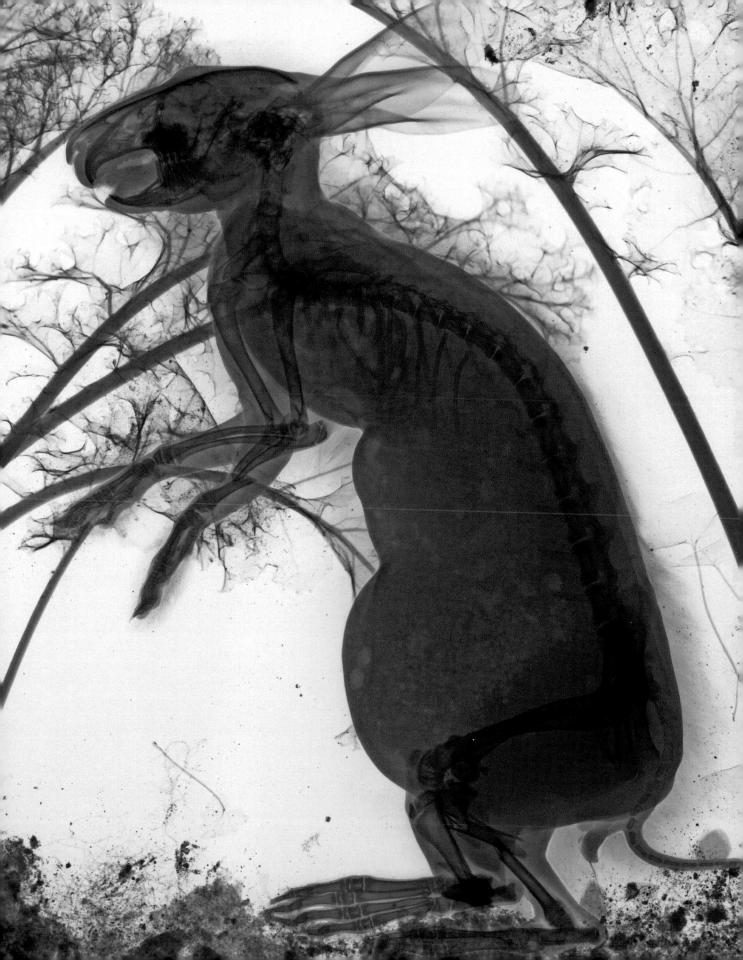

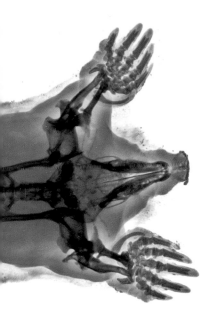

THE MOLE
Mammals never have more than five fingers (even when they have six)

A long body, short legs, pointed nose: the mole is actually an underground dachshund. And that's how the mole likes it: if you had to spend most of your life plodding through narrow tunnels that you dug yourself, you wouldn't want to have long legs or a round body getting in the way, would you? So what does come in handy when you're underground? Big old paws for digging with, strong legs, and no lumps and bumps to get caught on things when you're crawling around. Seems like the mole has it all worked out, huh?

If you look closely at the X-ray photo of the mole's paw, you can count not five, but six fingers. That hook coming out of its wrist is a sort of extra thumb. It doesn't move, but it does create a larger surface area. That helps the mole scoop away more earth when digging. But mammals are descended from animals with five fingers and toes on each of their hands and feet. Humans, mice, bats, bears, and many, many other species all have five digits, just as they should. Sometimes an unnecessary toe has disappeared, or the foot has turned into a hoof with even fewer toes. All of that can be explained. But one extra finger? How did the mole get that? Biologists scratched their heads for years over where that extra finger came from.

The extra finger does look quite different from the other fingers though. It's made up of one single bone, and it doesn't have a nail either. That's because it isn't a real finger—it's an overgrown wrist bone. Moles aren't the only animals with a fake finger. Pandas have one too. It comes in handy for holding bamboo. Ultimately, the paws of all mammals are put together in a similar way. You really have to hand it to Mother Nature.

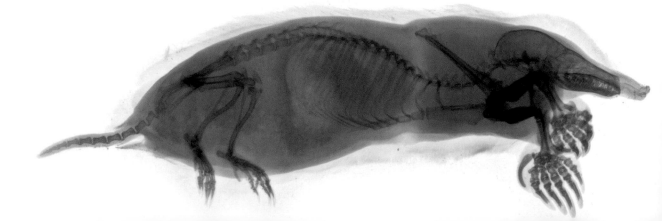

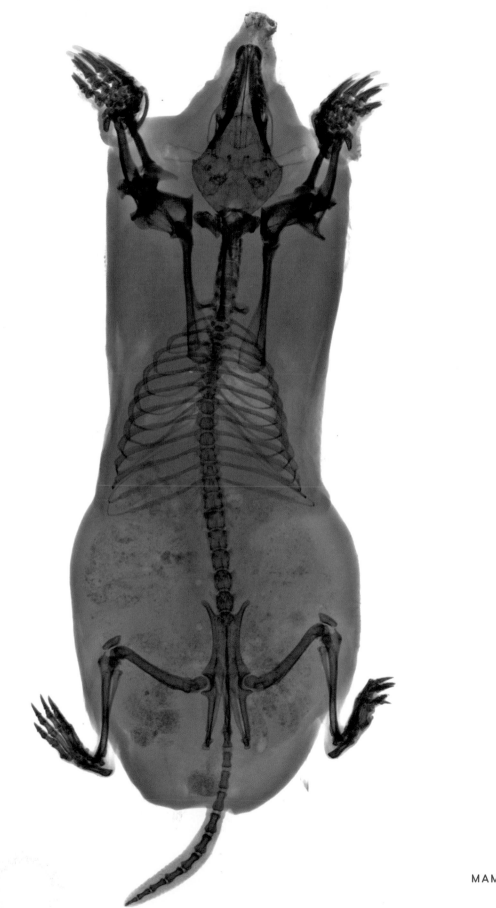

THE HEDGEHOG
A prickly mole

The X-ray photos of birds showed us that there is not much left of them when you take their feathers away, and now we're going to unmask the hedgehog as a bluffer too. Underneath all those prickles, hedgehogs are quite a bit smaller. They have pretty muscly backs though—but what good are back muscles? You can't run with them, you can't dig with them, you can't lift weights with them . . . But the hedgehog does have an important purpose for its back muscles: it uses them to make its prickles stand up straight.

The hedgehog's teeth, its pointed nose, and its short, strong legs make it clear that it belongs to same family of mammals as the mole. Hedgehogs don't dig underground. They stay on top of the earth and make their way through leaves, moss, and branches. There are more enemies above the ground than underground. That's why hedgehogs need their prickly protective layer.

It would be handy for hedgehogs if they had those spikes all over—they'd be less vulnerable, but it could also be pretty uncomfortable. It's a good thing they have a solution. Right where the prickles end, hedgehogs have a long, rounded muscle, like the elastic of a shower cap. If they're threatened by a predator, they tighten that muscle. When it pulls together, the prickly skin moves to cover the whole body. And all the predator sees is a spiky ball of hedgehog.

That's usually enough to keep hedgehogs safe, but foxes seem to have found a way around this protection. Some people say that foxes roll hedgehog balls into water, so that the little ball has no choice but to unroll. Others say that they pee on the rolled-up hedgehog, with the same result. A pee-covered hedgehog? That doesn't sound very tasty.

However, there are apparently people who sometimes eat hedgehogs too. Um . . . great. Well, at least they have a few thousand toothpicks, all ready and waiting.

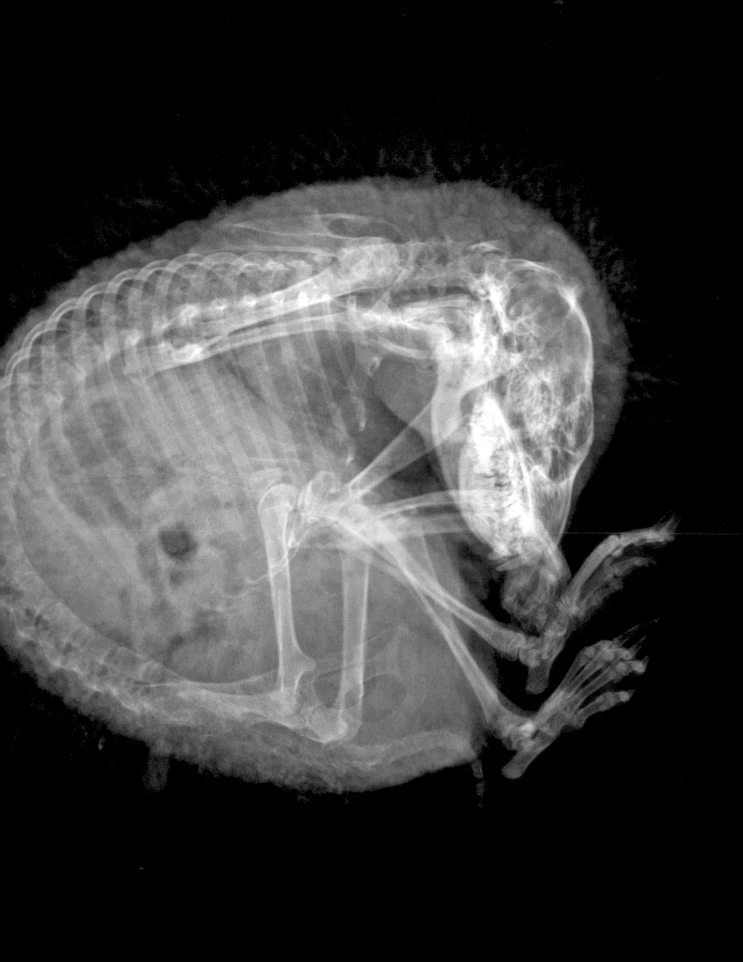

THE WEASEL

As wise as a weasel

Not rodent incisors, but canine teeth: that's a sign of a predator. And what a predator! Weasels even hunt animals that are bigger than themselves. Voles are their favorite food, but they also eat rats, moles, and even young rabbits and hares. Weasels have got some guts. They are super-hunters. A weasel can easily eat two mice a day. They have to, because they burn a huge amount of energy. They have to eat around a quarter of their body weight every day to make up for it.

By looking at their bodies, you can see how weasels hunt. Like moles, they have long bodies and short legs, so they feel perfectly at home in narrow underground burrows, and that is where they find their voles. Their victims stand virtually no chance against those deadly fangs. Weasels also have big claws that they can use as grabbers.

Weasels have a reputation for being sly and sneaky, and that's understandable. They're on the menu for a lot of creatures—from birds of prey to foxes and cats—so they need to be smart if they want to stay alive. And you have to be on the ball if you're hunting animals that are bigger than you. But that doesn't make weasels mean. They're simply alert and on their guard—which is very sensible. Perhaps it's time to change the saying "as cunning as a weasel" to "as wise as a weasel." Hey, it sounds better too!

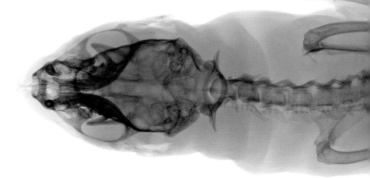

THE SQUIRREL
Handy little monsters

"It's all about what's on the inside, not what's on the outside": that's the advice many people will give you about love. You're better off with someone who's beautiful inside than beautiful outside. In that case, the squirrel should be a lot less popular with people than it is. When you take away that woolly coat and that fluffy tail, what's left behind looks like a monster. But it's a very handy little monster.

The squirrel's paws are like a monkey's hands. That allows it to perform gymnastics with the greatest of ease as it hops from branch to branch. You can also see that its leg bones are very sturdy. They have to be, because squirrels have muscular legs with really long feet that allow them to jump an incredibly long way. The bones need to be strong enough to absorb the shock of all those landings.

A squirrel's teeth are pretty impressive too. The bottom rodent incisors are not just there for gnawing. They can also be used like tweezers to work the smaller bits of nut out of a shell. Squirrels' teeth continue to grow throughout their lives, but squirrels gnaw on acorns and nuts every day, so their teeth wear out just as quickly as they grow. That's just as well, or squirrels might end up looking like walruses.

However, the most impressive thing about squirrels is, of course, their tails. They need that enormous tail to keep their balance when they're running along thin branches high up in trees. The tail works a bit like a tightrope walker's pole. And it's also handy for jumping. It allows the squirrel to adjust its direction in midair. Nearly all tree-climbing mammals have long tails. Squirrels are very cleverly constructed, from head to tail, inside and out.

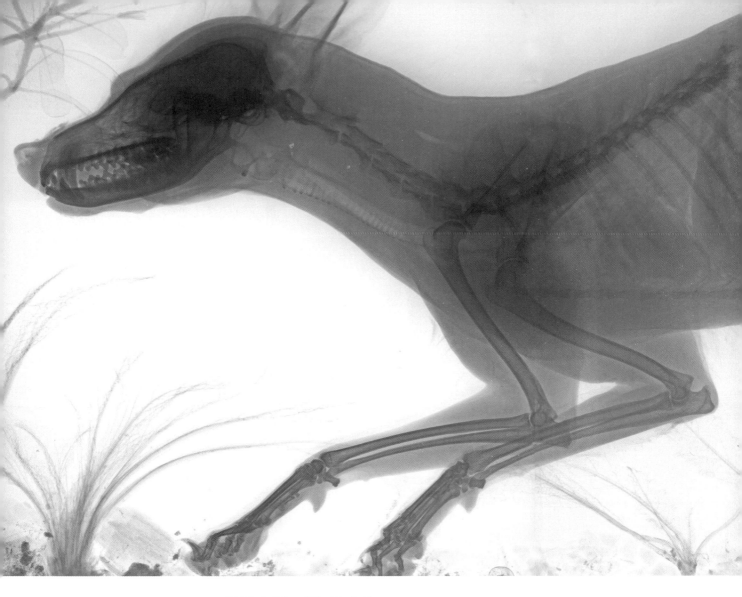

THE FOX

The tale of a tail

This animal could easily be a dog, or a wolf. But it's a fox. And it's clearly a male, if you see what I mean. But … why the long tail? Squirrels have long tails so that they can climb trees—but do you ever find foxes up trees? Well, yes, you do. Some foxes even sleep in trees. Can you see your neighbors' Labrador doing that? Maybe, because there are loads of videos of tree-climbing dogs online.

The tail also helps the fox to keep its balance when it's hunting and it needs to make a quick turn. And foxes communicate with their tails, too. For example, a high tail means "I'm in charge." And a low tail means the opposite, or

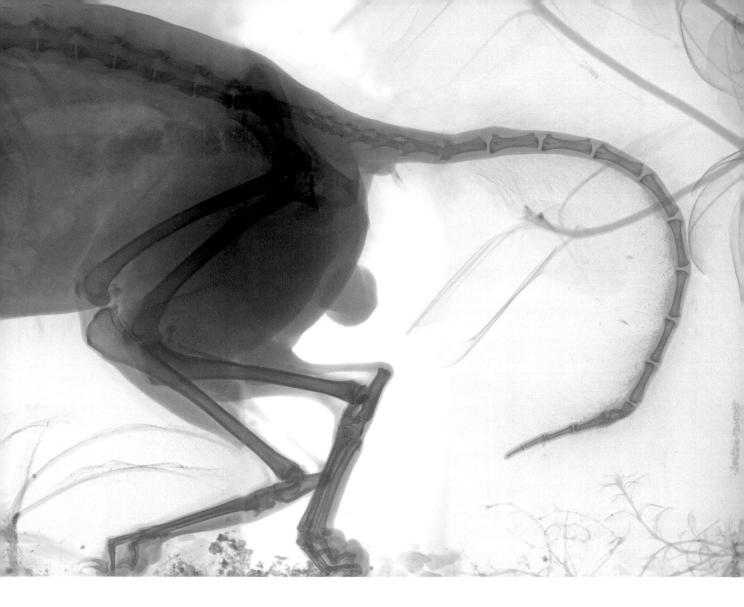

even fear. A fox also uses its tail for warmth. When it's cold, it will curl up and pull its tail over itself like a fur blanket.

Unlike wolves, foxes aren't that keen on running. They only do it when they're trying to get away. When hunting, they prefer to stalk their prey. Then they pounce. That's why their back legs are a little longer than their front legs. And their extra-long heel has a stronger muscle to give them more pouncing power. Using less energy and more brains to find your food—they're smart creatures, those foxes.

THE DEER
Living skeletons

Oops. We're almost at the end of our book full of bones, and there's a load of important information about bones that we haven't mentioned yet. But this X ray photo is a great opportunity to look at a few more bone facts. What you're looking at here is a very young animal. It looks like a newborn calf that's sleeping. However, this isn't a baby cow. It's a fawn, a baby deer. You can see very clearly that its bones are not "finished" yet. They need to grow together, particularly at the joints. There's still lots of soft cartilage there, which you can barely see in this X-ray.

Just about all the bones will be much bigger when this deer is a full-grown adult. But bones are never really finished; they go on growing all your life. Once you're an adult they don't grow any bigger, but they do keep renewing themselves. Within a few years, all the bones of a human or an animal are completely replaced. All the old parts disappear and new ones come in their place. Bones are bursting with life. They actually keep you alive, and not just because they protect you and provide support for your muscles. Bones are also blood factories. Have you ever wondered where the blood in your body comes from? Well, it's from your bones. Every second, our bones make around a million new blood cells. Bones also store calcium and other important minerals. If your body happens to have too much of these minerals at some point, then your bones store them up. When your body doesn't have enough, your bones release them.

Bones are also super-strong for their weight—much stronger than stone, steel, or concrete, for example. So be glad your bones aren't made out of some different material. Because then you would either be really heavy, or you'd spend way more time hopping around the hospital's emergency room than in the schoolyard. So we should be really happy with the skeleton we have.

Thank you, bones!

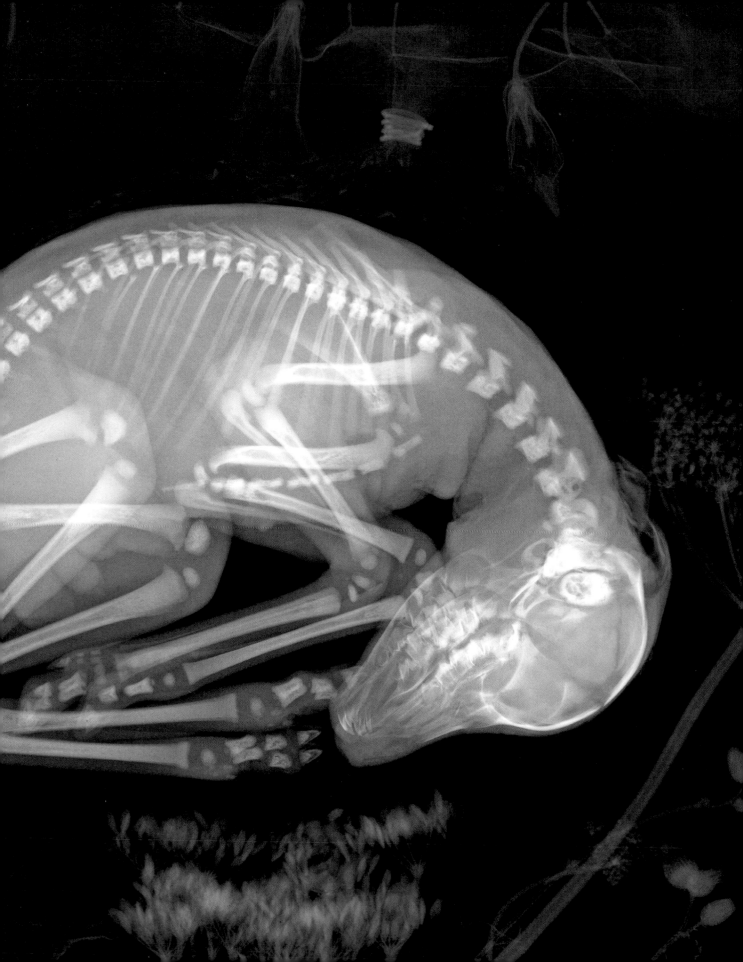

THE SQUIRREL MONKEY
Monkey brains!

From this photo, you can easily see how this animal got its name. Doesn't it look a lot like a squirrel, sitting up there in the tree? Like the squirrel, this monkey is a keen tree-climber, so it needs a long tail to keep its balance on those high branches.

You can see that, with this animal, we've come very close to human beings now. Okay, humans don't have tails. Even the great apes, like the chimpanzee and the bonobo, no longer have tails. And you can also tell from the short legs and the long body that this animal is not a human. However, it's inside the skull that you'll find the most important difference between humans and monkeys.

In general, you can say that the size of the brain determines how intelligent an animal is. So we humans have enormous brains. But elephants and whales have much bigger brains than us, so does that make them smarter? No. It all depends which part of your brain is biggest. And you can see in this photo that the front of the monkey's head—where it really matters—is smaller than in a human.

Inside the brain, there's an area known as the reptilian brain. This is very important for keeping us alive. Everything you do but don't need to think about—like keeping your heart beating, breathing, and the regulation of your body temperature—is controlled there. Around that is the mammalian brain, also known as the limbic system, the part that governs your emotions. Reptiles don't have this part of the brain. You can tell your turtle the best joke you know, but it's never going to laugh. With dogs, cats, and other mammals, though, you can clearly see what kind of mood they're in.

The outer part is the human brain, the neocortex. That's the part that's mostly missing in this squirrel monkey. Most mammals have only a thin layer of it, but humans have a huge layer of brains there. And that's the part that makes us so special. Because that's the area of the brain that we use for learning languages, for coming up with recipes like pizza quattro formaggi, for doing math, and for designing rockets to fly into space. Even in whales and elephants, that part of the brain is much smaller. That's why the first earthling on the moon was a human and not an elephant.

So, now you know it all. Except for one thing: how X-rays were discovered.

About the inventor

One day in November 1895...

"Go on, Anna," the German scientist says to his wife. "Put your hand there and make sure you don't move it."

"I'm scared," Anna replies. "And it's so dark in here."

The scientist smiles. "I promise you nothing will go wrong," he says. "It's not going to hurt. You won't feel a thing."

"Do I have to take off my ring?"

"No, you can keep it on."

"Fine. I'm ready."

"Really?"

"Really. No. Um... yes."

"Are you sure?"

"Yes."

"Good. Now... take a look at that screen."

"Huh? What...? What *is* that?"

"That, my dear Anna, is your hand. With your ring, on your finger."

"No!" shrieks Anna. "No! I've just seen my own death!"

It's hardly surprising that Anna was so shocked. Her husband, Wilhelm Conrad Röntgen, was taking one of the first X-ray photographs ever. Of her hand. On the screen, she could see every bone in her hand, and her ring, too. Her hand looked like a skeleton's. That would be enough to give anyone a shock.

In the weeks before, Wilhelm Röntgen had spent whole days in his laboratory. He had made an amazing discovery—completely by chance.

Röntgen had been researching radiation. Physicists had discovered that all manner of remarkable things happened with electricity. If you took almost all the air out of a glass tube and put two metal plates in there, applying a high voltage to the plates would cause beautiful colors to appear. But why was that?

Röntgen wanted to know the answer, so he did various experiments. During one of these experiments, he saw a nearby screen light up, even though there was no obvious source of light. The only object that could have been emitting rays was the glass tube, he concluded, but there was a cardboard case around it. So the rays must have passed straight through the cardboard and hit the screen some distance away. He'd never seen anything like that before. These were not ordinary light rays but something completely different—a kind of ray that could pass straight through objects. Röntgen held his own hand between the tube and the screen and saw "shadows" of the bones in his hand projected onto the screen. He had made the very first X-ray image.

After this discovery, he began to experiment. What else could the rays pass through? What could stop them? That was how Röntgen discovered that these X-rays, as he named them, could go straight through soft tissue but were stopped by hard material. It was this difference that made bones and teeth stand out so clearly against fat and muscles.

News of Röntgen's discovery soon spread all over the world. Röntgen won the Nobel Prize for his research, the most important scientific award you can receive. Other researchers set to work with his discovery, building even better X-ray machines. X-rays offered great opportunities for doctors: finally they could look inside their patients without cutting anyone open. Thanks to X-rays, security guards at airports can tell if someone is hiding banned objects without opening up their luggage. Archaeologists can study the inside of mummies without damaging them. Astronomers can use X-ray telescopes to study objects in space that do not give off light, but do emit X-rays.

And what about us? Well, thanks to Röntgen's discovery, we now know that long-eared owls are really scrawny little critters, that bumblebees have waspy waists, that bats fly with their hands, that the sole is a work of art, and that the inside often truly is more beautiful than the outside.

Index

The photographs in this book are the stars of the show, but there are also lots of fascinating facts in the text that will help you understand what you're seeing. This index will allow you to quickly find the information you are most interested in by showing you what pages to look for it on.

First published in Canada, the U.S., and the U.K. by Greystone Books in 2021
Originally published in Dutch in 2017 as *Binnenstebinnen: Röntgenfoto's van dieren*
by Uitgeverij J.H. Gottmer/H.J.W. Becht BV, North Holland, Netherlands

21 22 23 24 25   5 4 3 2 1

Greystone Kids / Greystone Books Ltd.
greystonebooks.com

Cataloguing data available from Library and Archives Canada
ISBN 978-1-77164-679-6 (cloth)
ISBN 978-1-77164-680-2 (epub)

Scientific review for the Dutch edition by Geert-Jan Roebers
Editing and indexing for the English edition by Catherine Marjoribanks
Proofreading for the English edition by Alison Strobel
Jacket and interior design for the Dutch edition by Steef Liefting
Cover design for the English edition by Sara Gillingham Studio
Interior design for the English edition by Fiona Siu

Printed and bound in China by 1010 Printing International Ltd.

Greystone Books gratefully acknowledges the Musqueam, Squamish, and Tsleil-Waututh peoples on whose land our office is located.

Greystone Books thanks the Canada Council for the Arts, the British Columbia Arts Council, the Province of British Columbia through the Book Publishing Tax Credit, and the Government of Canada for supporting our publishing activities.

This publication has been made possible with financial support from the Dutch Foundation for Literature.